A NEW RADICAL METAPHYSICS

Richard Schain

ISBN 978-0-9609922-9-4

ГП
Garric Press
Glen Ellen, CA

The ascent to the divine Life is the human journey,
the Work of works, the acceptable Sacrifice. This alone is
man's real business in the world and the justification of
his existence, without which he would be only an insect
crawling among other ephemeral insects on a speck of
surface mud and water which has managed to form itself
amid the appalling immensities of the physical universe.

Sri Aurobindo, *The Life Divine*, 2006

I dedicate this book to Melanie Dreisbach
whose bright spirit has immeasurably enriched
my life and work.

CONTENTS

A NEW RADICAL METAPHYSICS

PREFACE

I have prepared this new version of the *Radical Metaphysics* of 2002 because I consider the book to be my key work in which are contained all the principal ideas of my philosophical writings. There is a force and vitality here expressed that I do not think has been equaled in previous or subsequent books of mine. New concepts and revisions have been added. Nevertheless, the basic tone of the work has been maintained as well as its core concept—the need of a human being to create and develop his or her metaphysical self—his or her soul.

Sonoita, AZ, 2018

ORIGINAL PREFACE

In a certain sense, all my writings are long prefaces to the main effort of my project of thought—which has yet to appear in final form. It is, of course, apparent by now that it will never appear, that I will never reach its final statement. The four pieces included in this work have been written at different times and with somewhat differing styles, but the underlying theme is constant throughout—the task of building the metaphysical self that I have come to dimly see as a contribution to 'divinity', however one conceives that transcendental idea. This task has no end in the lifetime of any individual.

The problem of my interior life has always been the complete adherence of my milieu to the materialist worldview. There is no avoiding the fact that the social ambience of one's existence, one's *situation* (Sartre's French word), profoundly affects the life of the mind since there is no escaping the influence and acts of one's confreres. The idea of metaphysics is seen as the residue of primitive superstition, unworthy of an educated individual of the twentieth—now twenty-first—century. Opposing this idea has been the point of departure of my interior development. Virtually all of my writings (exempting a work on Nietzsche and my early medical career potboilers) represent my effort at developing a metaphysical consciousness. The meaning of this expression should become clear to anyone who dips into my work. Briefly, however, I regard a metaphysical consciousness to be a distinct form of being that is superior—I do not avoid the word—to material existence. One can envision how this belief has separated me, intellectually and emotionally, from the materialist-minded community into which I was born, raised, and educated.

It is not only the materialist world at large, however, which rejects metaphysics. The whole concept of metaphysics is out of synchrony with contemporary philosophical thought. Other than in the seminaries, there are few philosophers, particularly in the English-speaking world, who are willing to admit to a serious interest in metaphysical thought. Even more rejected is the dualistic mindset necessarily associated with metaphysics. Descartes, who was the father of modern dualistic concepts, has become the favored bête noire of philosophers. Metaphysics is in such poor repute that Paul Tillich, one of the most original philosophers of the twentieth century, whose writings are steeped entirely in metaphysical thought, felt compelled to reject the term metaphysics completely in his major opus *Systematic Theology*. He used the term 'ontology' whenever he meant metaphysics. However, terminology changes do not alter a basic situation. Tillich's ontology has as little contemporary acceptance as does metaphysics.

Since my writings are principally motivated by my own needs, one might wonder why I should anticipate that anyone else would take an interest in them. Why even should I care? I'm not sure I have satisfactory answers to these questions. However, I seem to gain pleasure from the thought that those with a metaphysical need, unsatisfied by conventional religions, may take some interest in my project of thought. It is interesting to find someone with a kindred spirit who makes known kindred thoughts. If, as Plato believed, knowledge is remembrance, my writings may help some remember that which has failed to gain entry into their consciousness. However, I do not shrink from the possibility that no one will ever have an interest in my writings. The real fulfillment for the person who generates an original philosophical work (I do not include histories, analyses, or critiques) is the process of bringing the writing into existence. Nothing else can even faintly compare to this in value for the soul of the writer.

Finally, I should say that the reader will find much repetition in these pieces. I do not apologize for repeating myself in matters bearing repetition. Repetition is a fundamental need for the development of the inner self.

Only through repeating myself over and over again, in varied ways, can I establish a new thought or a new value. Those who think repetition is a fault in writers do not understand the barriers to inner development—both for a writer or a reader. Repetition is the key to advancement of the metaphysical self.

Glen Ellen, CA, 2002

PRELUDE

Things don't work. That's the main point here, things don't work. I've been a good citizen most of my life, but things haven't worked. My eyes have slowly opened to the realization that things haven't worked. I've been lied to. I've followed all the rules, done all the right things, gotten the right education, met all the right people, married the right woman, had the right children, lived in the right neighborhood, had the right career—but things still didn't work. It's a heart-rending experience. I'm totally at sea and don't know where to turn. Something is rotten here; I'd like to clean out everything, decontaminate everything, especially kick all the liars out.

Through my mind's eye, the world has become a grotesque nightmare, an expressionist horror canvas. Everything is red and purple, bleached bones lie all around me, contorted figures have fangs dripping blood. What does it all mean? Why am I here? Where am I going? I am like an abandoned child, lost in a dark wood of ignorance and unhappiness. Something terrible has happened to me. I've been poisoned. People have been lying to me all the time. I've got to get away. But where can I go?

I can't ever forget how much I've been lied to, led astray, left in a dismal spiritual swamp. There must be something illegal about lying to people, especially young people. You can't lie to a woman about marriage; you get brought up on breach of promise. How much worse it is to lie to a young person, making him believe he will be happy if he lives his life a certain way. I must try to straighten myself out. *I must find the truth.*

Renewed from Schain, *Reverence for the Soul* (2001)

VISIONS OF A HYPERBOREAN

Hyperboreans write with their blood. Hyperborean writing is the blood of the soul. The image is not original with me but no matter, thoughts are common property of those who can make good use of them. Since I have never encountered anyone who has understood that my thoughts are the blood of my soul, my only recourse is to objectify them in writing so that I will not forget them and can nourish myself with them when the need arises.

The great event in my life has been my effort to create myself. By this I mean creating a soul, the metaphysical entity that gives meaning to all the miserable shuffling and struggling within low-minded societies that are hostile to the creation of a metaphysical self in an individual. I have found it necessary to continually rethink and reformulate my life; to go with the societal flow I find myself in would have resulted long ago in my spiritual drowning, an outcome which seems to me to have happened to most of my friends and relatives.

Consequently, it is my opinion that any individual who takes seriously his own existence as a human being, *Homo sapiens,* must cultivate a suspicion of the values of the society in which he lives. I live within the Euro-American society that dominates the world today; however, I cannot say I think it has ever been different elsewhere or at other times. There is just no recourse for the individual except to provide armor for himself against the unthinking crowds that always surround him.

This does not mean that I regard myself as a pessimist. On the contrary, life to me has been a remarkable adventure, one that I have not always been capable of facing squarely but never without great rewards when I have been able to master it. The development of a metaphysical self is a unique opportunity given to an individual who is capable of generating the necessary fortitude and energy to accomplish the task. What is necessary, first and foremost, is creating a direction for the self independently of that imposed by society. Once this has been accomplished, a whole new world of meaning emerges within the soul. I do not want to disturb myself unduly with the imprecisions of the English language in this area—soul, self, spirit, mind—all these refer to the various facets of interior being. *Geist* is what I mean if I may be permitted to fall back upon the more inclusive German term.

One must have a concept in mind in order to carry out sustained independent action. Otherwise, one becomes a lower-level organism reduced to the ping-pong existence of reflex living in a mechanical world. The concept I recommend is that of the *metaphysical self,* otherwise known as the soul. It is not a concept susceptible of precise definition in the materialist-scientific sense of the word. However, every mindful individual can become aware of the metaphysical self by considering his own being as a thinking, feeling creature. *Cogito ergo sum* is Descartes' statement of this concept, which, unfortunately, has never been carried to its ultimate conclusion. It is not only a proposition, it is a value statement that needs to be erected aloft on the banner of emergent metaphysical selfhood.

~ ~ ~

At this point, I feel compelled to dwell on the meaning of the word *Hyperborean* from which the title of this section has emerged in my mind. What does it mean to be a *hyperborean*? The term derives, as do many matters of the mind, from an ancient Greek legend describing a race of people living in the far northern, presumably Arctic regions. They were inaccessible by the usual routes of travel by land or sea. Pindar made reference to them and Nietzsche utilized the myth referring to his own life in a wonderful passage in *Twilight of the Idols*. It is a perfect metaphor for those aligning themselves to the metaphysical self in the present era. There is no acceptable route to the soul utilizing contemporary pathways.

There are two vices that can be poisonous for individuals who wish to make something of their interior selves. These are avidity for wealth and desire for love. They may appear to symbolize opposite poles of existence, but in fact, they both represent the same underlying weakness of the individual, the failure to develop reverence for his or her own soul. Both represent an escape from self, an inability to ground one's life on the only reality available, which is the interior self. Of these two vices, the need for love is the more dangerous since it is not recognized as a vice; whereas, most civilizations have known that material greed is detrimental to the self. The persistent need to be loved, in one form or another, is unrestrained throughout all levels of society.

It is the case with all vices that they cannot be dealt with successfully until they are replaced with an alternative reward which offers more to the individual than the vice in question. Vices can grow to huge proportions in those individuals with strong passions and with a will to express them. No one can free himself from the vice of greed until he comes to learn that the benefits of development of self outweigh the development of an estate. There has always been general awareness of this maxim; the problem now is that belief in the existence of the self has been eroded by the prevalent technological worldview.

By far the greater problem in western societies, however, is the belief that in the phenomenon of "love" is to be found the solution for the ills affecting the individual. There is no word in the English language that has been more abused and more subject to hypocrisy, confusion, and deceit than this term. The best approach would be to abandon it entirely, but this is not likely to occur given the long tradition of its usage. The ancient Greeks had numerous terms specifying the different meanings of the word: *eros*—erotic love, *agapé*—godly love, *philia*—friend love, *storgé*—familial love. In English language usage, one can love money, fame, family, a romantic partner, knowledge…the same word serves for all. Christian love (*agapé*) and erotic love (*eros*) appear to be completely antithetical concepts. There are even theologians who have claimed the word to be a synonym for God!

Nevertheless, close inspection reveals a certain logic to English usage. There is a common denominator underlying all meanings of the word *love* not evident at first glance. All these meanings have one property in common, which is the tendency toward *abandonment of the metaphysical self.* The moment one gives himself over to an emotion centered on an external object—no matter whether it is a thing, person, or abstraction—the interior self becomes impoverished; there is a loss of integrity, a loss of the vital reverence for self that is at the heart of successful living. A healthy orientation is replaced by a pathological fixation. Such a state of affairs is forgivable in a child or adolescent who is yet to enter into life's depths but it is a sign of inner decay in a mature adult. Affection, loyalty, and gratitude have their places in human affairs. Eros is a phenomenon that enriches life. However, "love" in all its unrestrained forms is a dangerous state of mind that can metaphysically damage unsuspecting individuals.

~ ~ ~

The principal advantage of hyperborean existence is the opportunity afforded for development of the interior self. One becomes able to truly assimilate the meaning of the ancient Greek injunction, "Become what you are!" To become what you are requires a prior state of mind in which there is a reverence for the soul. But before this reverence can be achieved, one must intuit that the soul exists. Here is to be found the great failing of the contemporary mindset in which one is persuaded that the soul or inner self does not exist. How can one revere what one does not believe exists? The hyperborean, however, is insulated from this error; encased in his igloo-like psychological solitude, his mind finds its own visions of reality and unlearns the naïve dogmas of the materialist viewpoint.

A vision is not the perception of what exists, it is of the future, of what one desires to come into existence. Living according to a vision is the essence of creative life as opposed to living as a slave or follower. The vision of creating the metaphysical self is the one thing necessary for a fulfilling life and to which all other visions or desires must give way. If this is not the central feature of a life, it becomes degraded into an ant-like scurrying about in an endless search for little morsels of *materia*.

It should not be necessary to specify that hyperborean existence is a state of mind, a metaphysical locale rather than a geographic site. However, being creatures of flesh as well as of spirit, there are considerations of the flesh requiring thought. Dues must be paid to the society in which one lives. But sooner or later, like a fledgling chick cracking the protective shell, the spirit must crack the protective shell formed by clan and country in order to become free for self-development. No matter how many protections and conveniences are offered, one's own homeland is a giant vise constraining metaphysical development. Every real person must become an *internal expatriate*—it is the necessary condition for a spiritually full life.

~ ~ ~

All the cards in the game of life are stacked against the individual with a desire to develop his interior self. Family and friends urge him in the directions sanctioned by the societal system. All the rewards, all the social warmth, all the security offered by the society in which he lives are predicated upon acceptance of the societal values, which in the 'developed' world of today are founded upon a materialist perspective with Christian socialist overtones. Reverence for the soul is an orientation bringing no social rewards. One can accumulate his fortune or work for his people, but endeavoring to develop a metaphysical self has little currency in a society accustomed to being able to weigh or measure all accomplishments worthy of note.

Yet, in the inscrutable scheme of things in which humans are required to strive and suffer, there is a saving grace that acts to equalize the game otherwise so heavily stacked against metaphysical development of the individual. This is the phenomenon of Angst so well known to those who have felt its force. Angst is the feeling that tells the individual he is sinning against himself when he accedes to the pressures of the social surround. Angst reminds him that there is more to life than playing out the program handed to him as a child when he was too young to know its meaning. Angst tells him that if he wants to be a man—or woman; there is no gender difference for the metaphysical self—he must look to himself to create the values by which he lives. Neither the acquisition of wealth nor the plaudits of those around him will provide him with these values. The foremost reality in the life he leads is to be found within himself; there is where he must expend the powers with which an unknown providence has endowed him.

It must be admitted that not many people feel the degree of Angst required to withstand social pressures. Democracy is certainly not a principle conducive to this capacity. With his perceptive insight, Schopenhauer expressed the view that religion is the metaphysics of the people; to this judgment can be added the proviso that religion is not confined to ecclesiastical systems, that there are also religions of wealth, of family networks, of charitable functions, of athletics and entertainment, and so on encompassing all the values espoused by societal systems and disseminated by the media. The Angst stemming from a neglected self is the faintest of feelings in many good soldiers of societal systems.

But, as an eminent thinker once said, "The crowd is always wrong." The one essential requirement for life suitable for *Homo sapiens* is reverence for the soul.

~ ~ ~

My style of life is to look within rather than without. I am not one to try to dominate my surround in an aggressive manner. There is little will to power, fame, or riches evident in my literary activities. However, I believe my way has *meaning*. I can see no purpose to life other than evolving an interior self through thought. All the emphasis I see on interactive living is circular, one lives to affect others who themselves live to affect others and so forth. The behavior is meaningless. The fruit of human life is in individual development; otherwise we really do live in an absurd universe.

There is no "proving" the existence or the meaning of the metaphysical self in any scientific sense; one must possess the intuition that it is so. One needs to strive to clarify and solidify this intuition. It emerges from the depths of consciousness; there are no revelations, no divine messages, no sacred traditions to sustain it. Its recognition, however, leaves one no escape from believing that it is an authentic apprehension of reality.

An illusion is belief in an idea about the material world that lacks reality. Ideas relating to the object world of *materia* are susceptible to confirmation through the usual methods. Development of these methods has led to domination of the world of nature, with impending catastrophic results. It is ideas about interior being not susceptible to instrumental confirmation that are so missing in the present time. Personal development does not occur without such ideas or intuitions to guide it. If things continue as they are, human beings will become indistinguishable from thought-processing machines and they will be relegated to the insect world by some higher form of life that must inevitably appear.

But perhaps this will not occur, perhaps the unmistakable drive toward individuality will assert itself more forcefully in which selves will be distinguished from their social surround, selves that are microcosms of thought in the midst of a vast material macrocosm. This is still the distinctive human difference from other forms of life; rather than swarming like bacteria, they differentiate themselves in a metaphysical manner.

The basic choice becomes evident to clear-eyed individuals. It is to make either spirit or *materia* preeminent. If valuing the spirit is an illusory value, then all that remains is biology, tribalism, and maintaining the species. Interior concerns become merely vanity, self-delusions created by hyperactive brains. Food, shelter, reproduction, politics, acquisition of material goods—these are what really count. In the rest of nature, it is abundantly evident that the species is everything, the individual nothing. The vaunted human consciousness then turns out to only be a survival mechanism. One struggles to reproduce and to maintain the family, race, country, humanity—however one envisions the social surround. The high point of individuality is retirement when the individual is too indoctrinated and too old to make something special of himself. Who would wish to live such an existence?

The important power-mongers of the world today seem to have largely accepted the materialist vision of the way things are. Thus, all the emphasis on interconnectedness, globalization, democracy, and "oneness" of the world. If they turn out to have a wrong worldview, a view fundamentally at odds with the human condition, they will have for no good purpose abandoned the birthright of a metaphysical self.

~ ~ ~

What is the feeling, thinking, willing metaphysical self? Is there a demonstrable reality corresponding to the concept? There surely is, it lies in the consciousness of self, a type of demonstration more substantial than the restricted probes of science into measurable phenomena. The concept may be absent in the mind but, nonetheless, its anlage is always there. Hence the ever-present possibility of Angst reminding the individual of its presence.

Every individual needs to chart his own route toward realization of the metaphysical self. No apostle, no saint, no canonical tradition, no organization of any type, no matter how it may be decked out in spiritual trappings, can serve as a guide to this end. The task cannot be fulfilled in its totality; individuals are only equipped to form their interior selves to a partial degree. However, one thing can be said with assurance, it is that ignoring the metaphysical anlage will result in a failed human life no matter how much exterior acclaim or material wellbeing is obtained.

The question of values is the key. One chooses between self-development, i.e., development of the metaphysical self, or exterior development in society with its current technological emphasis. If one does not *value* the soul, does not see its development as the one thing needful, is not willing to sacrifice for its sake, he will not be able to choose correctly. The opportunity for creation of a metaphysical self will have been missed.

~ ~ ~

The dirty little secret of modern times is that no one, not even the most 'spiritual' leaders of the numerous fee-for-wisdom organizations dotting the entrepreneurial spirituality landscape, believe in the existence of the soul. Neurophilosophers and neuroscientists dabbling beyond their depth have persuaded the intellectual world that it is the brain that counts, and that metaphysical beliefs, while possibly helpful for the unenlightened, represent a primitive holdover from eras lacking the insights of neurophysiology. It is the three-pound gelatinous-like lump in the cranial cavity, which is the essence of *Homo sapiens* and which ultimately will reveal to scientists all the esoteric secrets of the human condition.

The conflict between the dualistic viewpoint and scientific monism is an ancient one dating back to the disdain of the idea-oriented Plato for the materialist-minded Democritus. Plato's views generally prevailed in the antique world and became the substrate for Christian metaphysical dogmas. Today, however, the situation is reversed. This is in no small way due to the domination of nature and miraculous accomplishments of a technologically based science, extending far beyond the mere theories of Democritus. The masses always love a conqueror, especially when it provides no end of material benefits.

But there has been a saving few who have realized the limitations of the materialist *Weltanschauung*. One of the most notable of these was Arthur Schopenhauer, whose principal accomplishment was to put dualism into a more philosophically coherent framework by distinguishing between the world as will (i.e., soul) and representation (i.e., *materia*). He wrote about a great many other things that unfortunately detracted from his single important insight—as is often the case with assertively brilliant personalities. Furthermore, he confused his own thesis by repeatedly referring to representations as "phenomena of the brain," a contradictory statement on his part. Nevertheless, he got the main point right with his insight into the fundamental difference between self and world and its implications for the individual. No one has ever equaled him in his capacity to ridicule the naiveté of scientists who think their laboratories allow them to penetrate into the nature of reality.

Today, Schopenhauer has been largely relegated to a paragraph or two in university textbooks of philosophy while 'neurophilosophy' is an important feature of the contemporary intellectual landscape. All this is discussed in great detail in the section entitled *The Will to Metaphysical Existence*; however, repetition of an important point is valuable. Intellectual history needs remembering; one should not forget to mention Schopenhauer in any discussion of the distinction between *materia* and the metaphysical self.

~ ~ ~

Anyone with an interest in soul, mind, spirituality, self, etc. has no business talking about the brain. It is the ultimate sin of philosophy referred to by Aristotle as a *metabasis eis allo genos*, a passing from one realm to another. Just as Aristotle states that one cannot prove that a straight line is the most beautiful of lines, so one cannot demonstrate the meaning of metaphysical judgments by recourse to brain anatomy. It is a passing from one level of reality to another, a step leading not to knowledge but confusion. The problem is, however, that the materialist worldview recognizes only one realm of existence, that of the physical, and thinks other realms to be ultimately reducible to one single system. Woe to the civilization that does not recognize different realms of existence because it is doomed to shallow materialism and a society of materialists!

Some science pundit has recently defined humanity as an odd mold found on the surface of an insignificant speck of matter in the universe. This was not meant facetiously, this is the natural consequence of the monistic worldview. The insignificance of the individual human being becomes impossible to overstate. Here is to be found the real basis of materialism, consumerism, and many other "isms" plaguing contemporary societies—a total devaluation of self as a metaphysical entity. Inevitably there arises the compulsion for external acquisitions or connections to enhance the significance of the individual. But how can real significance be possible without cultivation of one's own soul, the metaphysical self? How sheep-like are those human beings who sell their souls for a mess of technological pottage!

The mind-body problem is the essential element affecting the mindset of the society even if most have little awareness of its nature. Once one accepts that the basis of the self is material in nature, that it is a clay-like lump in the cranial cavity, then an entire series of natural consequences are forthcoming. Material possessions are what count, experiences are physical in nature, life is a material affair. The way to enhance the self is through food, drink, drugs, and acquisitions of all kinds. Sensual stimuli are all important. The contents of the mind are of little significance in their own right, it is only their material consequences that are significant. When one hears that Socrates told an interlocutor that he feared to do wrong because his soul would be *damaged*, it is as if he were relating a fairy tale or homily for children. No one today takes such a thought seriously. More understandable in our world is the view of Epicurus who counseled against wrongdoing because one would always fear the consequences of discovery.

~ ~ ~

The joy of hyperborean existence is that one takes metaphysical thoughts *seriously*. The bottom line is the state of one's soul, not one's net assets. It is important to absorb—I say absorb not merely read—the thoughts of metaphysical writers like Schopenhauer or Nietzsche because they remind us how flimsy is the worldview of modern-day materialism. The concept of the metaphysical soul can be questioned but even the questioning lifts one out of the vulgar morass of scientific-technological existence. One is required by Nature to eat, defecate, copulate, and protect oneself from harm, but to elevate such activities to worship status?... The entire hedonistic, entertainment-oriented society is founded on this worship. Should it be shaken, who can say what cataclysmic events will be forthcoming—or what new forms of society may emerge.

The essential key to understanding the meaning of the mind's thoughts is to be found in language. *Words*— they have fascinated thinking individuals from Heraclitus to Sartre. The health of the soul is dependent on its proper relationship with language. To be understood properly is the dream of every person who takes his own soul seriously. Who is the one that is to understand the metaphysically minded thinker? First and foremost, it is himself, because without an understanding of self, there is little of value to communicate to the external world. It was not for nothing that the epigram in the temple at Delphi, which impressed Socrates so much, stated *gnothi seauton*, know thyself. This knowledge, however, requires the utilization of language.

As is usual in a technological society, technicians have dominated this area. Neurologists and linguists are the experts in language to which most people defer. However, it is not neurology or linguistics that the soul needs, it is the awareness that self-development and communication require a knowledge of language. The knowledge of more than one language is a metaphysically-enhancing capability. This may require a functional brain, but what is more important, it requires an orientation to the meanings language can impart. The ancient Greeks did very well with language without knowing anything of neurophysiology or having elaborate syntactical theories. What they did have were metaphysically significant human beings who had something of consequence to say and others who valued their expressions.

Somewhere Friedrich Nietzsche says that the soul is just another word for the body. Now what Nietzsche has to say is always of interest even if he was too much affected by his tortured relationship with his society. I would like to invert his sentence and say that the body is just another word for the soul. It is its exterior face manifesting itself as an apparatus for relating to the world. There is no point trying to find a specific contact between the metaphysical and physical self because by now it is clear that it is beyond human capacity to discover it. We are the incomprehensible mix of "fire and clay" eloquently described by William James. Some inscrutable providence has composed our race so that a few prefer fire while most seem to prefer clay.

~ ~ ~

At seventy years of age, I feel myself to be at the zenith of my conceptual powers. However, my body is clearly declining in every one of its functions. If this is not conclusive evidence of a mind-body dichotomy, then I don't know what else can be said. "The thing speaks for itself" is a legal proof whose Latin equivalent I can no longer remember. One day my mind will disappear when my brain can no longer sustain its activity. The personality known as Richard Schain will be gone. The tragic fate of every soul-spirit-mind-self-psyche consists of the decline of the body that relates it to the material universe.

I consider it shockingly blasphemous for a mature *Homo sapiens* to try to extend the reality of his soul beyond the space-time dimensions that limit his life. "Immortality" of the soul is an arrogant idea having no place in a serious philosophy of life. If Kant had been more consistent, he would have consigned this idea to the dustbin of cultural history. Instead, he supported it for the flimsiest of reasons. The whole idea is infantile—its perpetuation in western history is due to the self-serving posturing of clerics. The human soul is part of human life, when life is over the soul retreats back from whence it arose—something that is beyond the ken of human knowledge, like the dimensions of the universe or the end of time. Meanwhile, the care of the soul during life is manifestly the responsibility of every individual possessing metaphysical powers.

What is the importance of all this metaphysical hobnobbing? It is to make clear that scientific materialism is a secondary affair in the human condition, a tinkering with the nuts and bolts of material existence underlying the main drama—the development of the metaphysical self. It is the health of his soul, not his body, which is the key issue for a human being. It does no good to pamper the body while the soul decays. Anyone who does not grasp this essential fact and respond to its implication is at the mercy of a technological society indifferent to human spiritual welfare.

An essential distinction to be made by the metaphysical mind is between *analysis* of concepts and *choice* of concepts. The former has been entirely the rage for some time and is what happens in academic philosophy. Analytic thinking is important when it is a question of designing a nuclear reactor or discovering a cure for cancer. However, when it is a matter of advancing one's own metaphysical condition, advancing one's soul—which is what every human psyche should strive toward—then the choice of concepts becomes paramount. *Values,* in other words, are what must be embraced; in this effort, scientific thinking is of no value, there is no such thing as a science of personal values. One thing can be confidently asserted, if the individual does not choose his own values, his society will impose the prevailing ones upon him.

~ ~ ~

Science as the Will to Power—The 'progress of science' is the concept underlying the direction of western civilization. It proceeds in the following manner: some clever, highly-trained, success-minded individual discovers some new aspect of the natural world and envisions ways of utilizing it for practical purposes. Other clever, highly-trained, success-minded individuals bring into being techniques for actualizing the utilization of these new discoveries. Still others discover methods of persuading people that these discoveries represent advances in the quality of life. Money is exchanged and a new device is introduced into public life. Of course, those who have no money are left out and feel deprived.

An effort was made by the most prescient philosopher of the nineteenth century to elaborate the thesis that the "will to power" underlies the activity of all living creatures, including humans. Without feeling the need to defend this thesis as the ultimate explanation of life, it is surely true that it is a fundamental feature of life in general and human life in particular. Nietzsche made the case that it was behind the religious impulse in European societies. That insight was an important development in his era. Today, however, it is more important to recognize that scientific progress represents a will to power by its innovators. This recognition is necessary to have a clear view of the relationship of all forms of science to one's own life.

There is a manifest force behind the inexorable movement of science into all aspects of daily life. No acute observer of the development of modern societies can possibly miss noticing it. 'Technological Progress' is the term that promoters of development use to label this force but this is merely a label, devoid of information. The questions that need consideration are what is the nature of this force and how does it affect the soul of the individual. The first of these questions seems to have a simple answer for those with eyes to see; the force stems from the will to power of the entrepreneurial individuals behind scientific progress. This may not necessarily be crude economic power, although this surely plays a role, but is principally the psychological power deriving from determining the direction of society. He who can persuade people to desire the products he invents or produces has more power over society than the most brutal of dictators. The pervasive analytic attitude that is the basis of scientific technology permits this process to proceed full steam ahead and it is proceeding as might be expected. The advances of science are not charitable affairs or results of investigative curiosity but represent the will to power of the technicians and scientists.

The second question, however, is a more difficult one, especially since the purveyors of progress have convinced most of the world that the soul does not exist. What does not exist is of no concern to them. But souls do exist and their neglect results in the profound *dehumanization* seen everywhere. What has been gained in controlling nature by technological means has been lost in the deterioration of the metaphysical self. There is a vague premonition of this decay lurking in the most unexpected places amidst the rich and famous. It is the basis of the Angst that plagues many who still possess remnants of a soul. Some turn to traditional religions in search of solace, others to various worthy movements, but nothing outside substitutes for development within.

Those who still possess a regard for their souls need an ironclad defense against the assaults of a society that has no regard for the metaphysical self. Nothing can be believed, no traditions accepted, no contemporary standards taken at face value. Everything must be reassessed according to the values of the individual who wishes to save his soul. It is useless to prescribe prescriptions for this process; prescriptions should be left to the medical profession who spew forth drugs like police pouring forth tear gas to control a crowd. The individual needs to look to his inner self, he needs to develop the metaphysical capacity called *intuition* (read the forgotten Henri Bergson) and elaborate the standards that will firmly establish the metaphysical self. This may be the most hyperborean of visions but it is one that is supported by the human need for metaphysics.

There is no end to scientific progress because there is no end to the will to power of those who have mastered its levers. This is the *bad infinity* described by Hegel and referred to by Kierkegaard. The constant elaboration of methods to master the physical universe has an opposite effect upon the metaphysical self. Asceticism and solitude, the necessary tools of inner development are the antithesis of progress as conceived by the power-mongers of society. Once the necessities of life are mastered, further material progress not only does not develop the soul, it drains the energies that are required for spiritual development. (Spiritual—a word hijacked by theologians but one necessary to recover for the benefit of *Homo sapiens*.)

A certain spiritual immobility exists in those whose lives are devoted to material progress. Reality for them lies in the accumulation of objects, reports of instruments, or perusal of computer data. There is no attention to the report of the interior self. It is tragic to see so many energetic and talented individuals sell their spiritual birthright for the lures of scientific activity and the affairs of business. The greatest impediment to personal development is this obsession with "progress" and the acquisition of material goods. Where is the technological revolution and its globalization leading the human race? Yet it appears that all the benighted societies of the world are struggling to follow the lead of their more technologically developed neighbors. A seer is needed to discern the future. Or perhaps the future is clear but one resists seeing it...the robotization of the human species.

There is a clear dichotomy between the will to material power (in which fame and riches are subsets) and the will to self-development based upon reverence for the soul. I regard the latter as a superior manifestation of the phenomenon of human life. *Reverence for the Soul*—the key to an enhanced position of the individual in the cosmic scheme of things.

~ ~ ~

Egoism of the Soul—An inordinate egoism is needed for the soul to develop its potential. With all the best intentions in the world, it is impossible to develop an interior self without a powerful will to overcome the thousand and one problems that life and society impose upon the individual. To permit the will to self-development to flag is a formula for death of the self. It is better to die early than to have death creep up before the vital functions are actually extinguished. This was the credo of Jack London—live meteorically, live life with new experiences and new insights. One has to avoid living on the capital of the past, which necessarily gives out at some point. When the individual begins to concentrate on his comforts, health, and security, something needs to be done to rejuvenate his spirit.

A life of pure relaxation, no matter how filled with sentimental nonsense, is merely waiting for biological death. The crowded condition of the planet can ill afford the luxury of supporting too many such vegetative entities. Better any kind of purposeful activity, even the most apparently senseless, than none at all. Better to make errors than to do nothing. Better to use up one's energy than to wait passively for who knows what. Age can be overcome; the current Pope has referred to the perennial youth of the human spirit in connection with his own eightieth birthday. This is one area where one may profitably follow the lead of the Holy Father.

I do not accept that my life has been mediocre even though society may judge I have accomplished hardly anything worth noting. I have kept myself alive and sane for a decent interval while paying dues to my society—but as much could be said of most of the six billion souls currently inhabiting the planet. I recognize there is nothing externally distinguished about my life. However, I know that I have created myself as a unique metaphysical being who has risen above the domain of culturally-determined creatures. I have distinguished myself in the realm of spirit even though those around me may think this claim to be absurd. Beyond all the societies on earth, I believe there is a transcendent reality of spiritual being of which I am an important part. I have my niche within this reality. No human being should wish for more.

The greatest events and the most powerful of experiences consist of bringing significant thoughts into consciousness. All the world's activities are trivial compared to this phenomenon of the mind. What does the superior person (dare I say *Übermensch*?) actually do? He thinks superior thoughts and enhances his soul—that is the mark of his superiority. His activities may be judged one way or another; they are of value only to the degree that they help develop his metaphysical self.

Anything that is conducive to an individual thinking well is good; everything else has relative degrees of badness. The problem of American society is that individuals are conditioned to believe that actions are the hallmark of the good life. Thomas Edison and Henry Ford, not Emerson or Thoreau, are the heroes of American culture. And from there, it is only a short step to conclude that material acquisitions are the choicest fruit of actions. Thus, one enters into a technologically based society. Actions or acquisitions, however, no matter how personally or socially desirable, are valuable only to the extent that they enlarge the conscious mind of the doer or acquisitor. As soon as they lose that property, one might as well consign them to the ashcan. But technology seems to act upon the world population as alcohol did upon primitive American Indians. There is no using it in moderation for beneficial purposes; it is carried to excess until there is evident damage to the interior self.

As far as doing good for others is concerned, I have yet to see any do-gooder who is capable of contributing to the spiritual development of his recipients—the only type of development that is worth mentioning.

~ ~ ~

Megalomania of Self—The lack of a genuine self-respect of a reverence for the soul is what leads to the obsession with extending the self beyond its normal bounds of time and space. Historically, one of the crudest forms of this obsession can be seen in the efforts of the Pharaohs of

Egypt to construct gigantic structures filled with the most sumptuous goods to carry their souls to the nether world. Christian beliefs emphasized more spiritual approaches to the illusions of immortality, but created no less ridiculous ideas about the soul's ascent or descent to paradise or hell according to circumstance. Similar ideas exist in most organized religions, especially Islam. Kant in his otherwise epoch-making *Critique of Pure Reason* concluded that belief in immortality was such a fundamental feature of the human psyche that it had to be accepted on faith alone.

These gross historical instances of megalomania of the self can be greatly enlarged by including more modest examples from ordinary life. Preoccupation with enduring fame, with generational continuity, with survival of one's works after death, with endowing monuments expected to perpetuate the memory of the endower are common examples of the obsession with transcending the limits of one's own area in time and space. It seems as if we humans cannot be content with our own lives, we must project them into the vast multidimensional spaces surrounding us. In this, we go far beyond other forms of life that confine themselves to procreational activity.

Why is this so? I maintain it is a consequence of the failure to develop an adequate regard for self that would be sufficient to meet the needs of the most ambitious of individuals. It is a great privilege to lead the life of a sentient human in societies that provide the essential physical infrastructure for living. The most diverse forms of experience and expression are open to the individual who makes use of his opportunities. Most importantly, every human being possesses an inner potential known as the soul with which he can develop his unique personality. The moment of existence encompassing a human life would be more than enough to satisfy any individual if he became conscious of his resources and *valued* his interior self.

The disbelief in and devaluation of the soul that is the product of scientific-technological thinking is largely responsible for the prevailing lack of satisfaction with self. One who conceives of himself as just another mechanism in a world of mechanical entities will never have a reverence for his inner self. But his soul will still be within him in incipient form, constantly crying out for recognition. Unlike Heine's mechanical man who was never given a soul, there is no creator to whom he can complain. The failure to become conscious of his own soul, which translates into a failure of its development, leads to the obsessive need to project the failed self beyond its natural confines. The striving for power, fame, personal immortality, group identifications, social accomplishments, and so forth, are all indicators of a sickly soul. They represent a wrong direction in life because they are not founded on the reality of the metaphysical self. The here and now of the interior self is the only arena within which the individual can reliably expect to find his fulfillment.

~ ~ ~

I and the Object World (Dualism)—Those who say that the soul is just another name for the body confuse themselves with semantics. Dualism is an orientation toward reality, not a definition of it. If the Christian idea of soul referring to a part of the self detachable from the body is the concept at hand, than one may object saying all evidence indicates that body and soul are different aspects of the same underlying reality and do not exist apart from each other. But unbending monists view the soul as an illusion arising from neural activity; a very different concept of the unity of mind and body. This seems to be the attitude of the mandarins of western science. One thing is certain, the meaning of the human condition will never be elucidated via neurophysiology.

The very word "dualism" today has a pejorative implication. A dualist is thought to be someone whose mind is not sufficiently developed to realize that everything can be explained on a materialist basis; what science has not yet explained will be explained at a future time when the technology to explain "metaphysical" mysteries will have been sufficiently developed. This idea dates back to the nineteenth century philosopher Auguste Comte who believed that philosophy was a mid-stage between religion and science, the latter representing the final development of human understanding of all aspects of a universal nature.

The ill repute in which dualism is held at the present time by intellectually-minded individuals is due to a misconception fostered by religious superstitions. There is no reason to think that there are two substances in the universe known as body and soul. The idea that spirit somehow exists "apart" from the material self is a poor idea that deserves consignment to the trashcan of intellectual history. Just as matter and energy have been finally recognized by physical science to represent two different phenomenal forms of the underlying reality, so brain and soul as viewed by observers are only two aspects of a unitary individual.

What dualism means—should mean—is that there is a fundamental division between one's perceptions of a material world obedient to natural law and the intuitions of self regarding one's own unperceived metaphysical existence. These intuitions are just as valid, just as true, and just as meaningful as the perceptions of the world of the senses. One of the works of the philosopher Nicolai Berdyaev is entitled, *I and the Object World*, misleadingly translated by a market-oriented publisher as *Solitude and Society*. However, the Russian title is a more accurate description of Berdyaev's ideas about the nature of reality. *I and the Object World*—if Berdyaev had not already preempted this title, I might have used it myself. It is a genuine hyperborean vision.

There is no reason to believe that the report delivered by the objective, analytic, instrumental domain of an unyielding science is any truer, more profound or meaningful than the report of a developed self. In fact, there is every reason to believe that it is a more superficial, meaningless, misleading report than that delivered by the subjective orientation of the "I." The one virtue of objective science is that it leads to an ability to control nature, thus strengthening the physical security and capacities of the individual. However, along with this control of nature comes its deformation, taking the individual down a dangerous path of tinkering with themselves and the ambient world.

It may be noted that there is a similarity of this exposition to the teachings of Vedantic scriptures elaborated millennia ago. *Brahman=Atman* is the Vedantic way of expressing the significance of the self. As a Jewish scripturist once noted, there is nothing new under the sun. This may be a natural concept for a Brahmanic society but those who have grown up in western culture cannot escape the deforming impact of the emphasis on technology. It is branded on Euro-American consciousness. We who derive from the traditions of the western world have to come to grips with this brand, both its positive and negative effects. There is no escape from the burden of culture, Berdyaev tells us; it must be shouldered with its full weight upon the individual.

To repeat, the dualistic point of view does not mean there are two different kinds of substance in the universe, rather there are two different ways of confronting it. Epistemologically, the thought is simple Spinozism. However, Schopenhauer was a more vigorous exponent of the idea and more attention needs to be paid to his emphasis on will instead of representation. The objective approach to things means concentration on their physicality. The advantage of this approach is in its (relative) predictability, thus nature can be manipulated to one's presumed advantage. The other approach is properly labeled "metaphysical" because it goes beyond the physical dimension. It has to do with the melange of intuition, emotion, and will that composes the inner reality of the individual. This is the far more *interesting* approach of the human condition, which inevitably seems superior to those who cultivate it. Nietzsche continues to be so interesting a century after his death because he so exemplifies this type of philosophical thought. Others may be more consistent and scholarly in their writings, but none write from their interior being as did Nietzsche.

The poet José Bergamin is said to have responded to a critic by saying, "If I were an object, I would be objective; as I am a subject, I am subjective." This is not a facetious remark, interior reality cannot be analyzed objectively without descent into the pointless babble that is so prevalent in scholarly discussions. The substance of a literary work will not be elucidated by grammatical analysis. The emotional impact of music is lost by confining oneself to a study of its instrumental techniques. Plato or Nietzsche cannot be reduced to tables of categories. The metaphysical sense of reality fundamentally differs from the material sense in that it arises from the inner state of the individual; when it leaves this locale, all its significance evaporates. There is nothing incorrect about the physical, objective approach to the existent world, it is just that it is shallow compared to that centered on metaphysics. What is gained in predictability is lost in profundity. Pushed to an extreme degree of objectivity, society becomes composed of talking robots with analytical machines. The distinctive human condition disappears.

~ ~ ~

Why is it that I am so much more attracted to nineteenth century literature than the twentieth century equivalents? Is it because the habit of dualistic thought, the valuation of the inner self has faded—or at least failed to find societal recognition? Where is a Thoreau, Emerson, Heine, Kierkegaard, Schopenhauer, Nietzsche, Strindberg in the twentieth century? Perhaps an exception was the tragic figure of Fernando Pessoa who was so far outside the mainstream of western thought that he should be regarded as a nineteenth century relic. Nor are there figures from the centuries preceding who catch my attention to a similar extent. I have to return to antiquity to find literary individuals who stand out in my mind.

There is an interior awareness present in many cultural figures of the 19th century that seems to disappear as the scientific-technological era gained momentum. I doubt if its like will appear for centuries to come—if ever. Western culture has paid the price for infatuation with mechanistic thinking; the price paid is loss of interior self. It is difficult for a generation that disbelieves in the soul to produce profoundly creative personalities.

Progress is an illusion of an era mired in *schlechte Unendlichkeit*—bad infinity. The human species seems to be predisposed to peaks of internal development punctuated by long periods of animal-like activity, albeit enhanced by technology. We live in the wasteland of a technological civilization best compared to the monument-building era of pharaonic Egypt. It is disconcerting to see what happened to Egypt after the Pharaohs.

History teaches, however, that it is wrong to think the metaphysical impulse will disappear completely. Those who expected religious institutions to collapse in the face of scientific advances have been proven to be bad prophets. Looking at the world as a whole, organized religions are more influential now than ever before. What may have been lost in secular authority has been more than made up for in influence on the attitudes of people everywhere. Metaphysical beliefs exist, as do the values deriving from them albeit they are often kept under wraps. Metaphysics for the people is a thriving industry.

~ ~ ~

Exoteric and Esoteric—One way of regarding dualism is to divide it into the exoteric and esoteric elements of human life. Ordinary day-by-day experiences are exoteric; they are the report that life is a mélange of sensations, some pleasurable, some painful. Science is by definition exoteric because it is based upon the report from the senses and its validity is confirmed by the same report, albeit greatly magnified by instrumental analysis. The report is available to anyone and those with a practical turn of mind can utilize it for practical purposes. The whole world of contemporary technology is founded upon exoteric reports causing the human condition at the turn of the twentieth century to be decidedly exoteric in its orientation. 'Sensationism,' literally interpreted, is the order of the day.

Nevertheless, there is also a persistent esoteric element in individuals arising from a consciousness of self and an awareness of the superficiality of the exoteric. Esoteric knowledge means intuitive knowledge, knowledge that is subjective in nature. The subject contributes more to it than the object. It reflects the metaphysical self more than it does the external world of *materia*. In order to develop esoteric awareness, it is necessary to limit the influence of exoteric stimuli that always threaten to crowd out the more fragile metaphysical phenomena. Henry David Thoreau's dictum, "Simplify, simplify, simplify" is far more essential today than it was in his time. Individuals cannot simultaneously orient themselves in both directions; the metaphysical aspect of existence usually gives way. While biological life requires some attention to exoteric stimuli, exclusive preoccupation with it will render one unfit for the profounder elements of human life. The brain becomes functionally disabled, so to speak, for supporting these elements.

One is not able to function in a world dominated by mechanical devices and mechanical values without a corresponding atrophy of the metaphysical self. There is a common reservoir of energy underlying all psychic activity; when it largely flows into exoteric living, little remains for what is within. Add to that the prevailing devaluation of unquantifiable phenomena and individual metaphysical development becomes all but impossible. The mind becomes habituated to causality-oriented lines of thought rather than the cultivation of self. Exclusive orientation to cause and effect relationships makes for a mechanical robot instead of a vibrant soul.

What I think truly horrible is the practice of permitting small children to daily interact with computer screens for hours on end. It is worse than television addiction, which is a purely passive activity. Stunting of the soul must result from this process because a growth period of any type is a period of vulnerability to noxious stimuli. One day the practice will be seen as analogous to sending children into coal mines or sweat shops in order to lead them into adult employment. But all this has been done and is done with the best of intentions. *O sancta simplicitas!*

If the tendency of the exoteric is to crowd out its alternative thought form, the tendency of the esoteric is to create an unsustainable personality. It has been long known that the most creative minds are subject to madness. The example of Nietzsche stands out the clearest. It may be that humans are constructed to function more readily in the exoteric dimension and that evolving the deeper aspect of the self puts a great strain on the total human organism. The individual can never totally dispense with input from the senses nor would this be desirable since one cannot develop in a closet. Life's experiences are required for inner development to occur. Thus spiritual ideas are often founded upon ritual, history, race, nationality, and gods in human form. The concepts of heaven, hell, and immortality are basically exoteric since they derive from physical space-time constructs. Every institution for esoteric thought incorporates a firm exoteric element. One need only survey the framework of most organized religions. In all these situations, the exoterica are always prone to take command.

One is forced to conclude that sustained esoteric— i.e., metaphysical—thought combined with an intellectual conscience maintaining contact with reality is possible for only a small segment of any population, a segment whose minds are capable of transcending the immediate world of the senses. Because many yearn for deeper experiences but few are capable of supporting them, a degree of exoterica is often introduced into metaphysical thought. Organized religions are metaphysics for the masses according to Schopenhauer. But those with an intellectual conscience and in full possession of their faculties cannot tolerate the contamination of the highest aspect of their souls.

~ ~ ~

It is necessary to admit that an exclusively esoteric attitude to existence deprives one of the most cherished human pleasures. The world is a pleasure-filled place. Its sights, sounds, tastes, and feelings produce marvelous feelings within the individual. Luscious erotic and culinary delights are everywhere. And the sexual sensations!—the exquisite fulfillment of passionate longings—require powers beyond mine for adequate description. It is no wonder that it is rare to wish for death even when one is *in extremis,* for to die is to give up forever the pleasures of living. Yet every thinking person knows his life requires more than pleasure. It requires him to create an inner self that goes beyond indulgence of the pleasure principle. If he does not succeed in this task, his life will have been a failure. This realization will haunt him to his end and no amount of pleasure will assuage his guilt.

There is no reason to enumerate all the experiences withheld from one who does not attend to the exoterica of society. The Stoic attitude is impractical today since the ancient Stoics could hardly have imagined the vast range of sensual and material temptations available to the modern man who can purchase them. The religious ascetic thinks to find in religious preoccupations a substitute for pleasures of the senses. There is no substitute for pleasures of the senses. It is a necessary phase in human development. Esoteric life is not suitable for the healthy young who require physical fulfillment in all its forms. There are good reasons for abandonment of the unnatural practice of shutting up immature youths in monastic institutions.

Nevertheless, there comes a time for many when the pressures of dualism are too great and a choice must be made. For some, the choice is not necessary; they are wedded to the exoteric life at an early age. But for others, the hard choice between career, wealth, family, and sensuality on the one hand and metaphysical development on the other must be made. To devote one's primordial energies to the esoteric aspect of existence requires a certain contempt for the exoteric elements of society; without this contempt, the renunciation required would be too difficult. *Contempt is the shield of the soul.* May I add my belief that institutionalized religious metaphysics is no improvement over an honest personalized contempt. Better a full-blooded materialism than puerile religiosity!

~ ~ ~

Will to Power—There is a clear distinction between the will to power (in which fame, altruism, and greed are subsets) and the will to self-development. I regard the desire to develop the self as a higher form of expression than that manifest by the desire to conquer the world, whether the conquest be in physical or mental arenas. "Reverence for self" is my key to a metaphysically distinguished life.

It is hard to ascertain why such credence is given to the belief that assertion of self as a part of a group is superior to assertion of self as an individual. It is so obviously a lower-level form of expression. Yet everywhere, there is the obsession with searching out of traditions and cultures, which essentially means the desire to revert back to the primitive group mentality. The identification may be religious, ethnic, national, linguistic, familial, occupational—the list is quite long. It is one thing to band together for a specific purpose in order to assure security or strengthen a capacity. It is quite another to prop up one's individuality through group identification. When it comes to development of the soul, every group is a retarding factor. Kierkegaard's dictum that the crowd is always wrong should be placed above the entry of all public gathering places, corporate structures, and institutions of learning.

Globalization of Souls—Even more than identification with groups, the globalization of technology tends to diminish the real self. The vastness of human knowledge and expertise that can be disseminated to anyone with the wherewithal to purchase them acts as a brake on personal development. As the computer-driven information age expands geometrically, exoterica crowds out the development of the soul. The latter appears to the object-habituated mind to be so insubstantial and unreal as to merit no attention. Walk into a well-stocked bookstore in order to gain the impression that everything has been discovered, everything objectified, everything expanded beyond the purview of the mere individual. It seems only necessary to familiarize oneself with the experience and knowledge gained by others. One feels the objectivization of the universe is the sole reality worthy of serious consideration. The interior self fades into oblivion.

The blind spot of the globalized mentality is the lack of awareness that the metaphysical self has a reality and a meaning transcending exoteric superstructures. The globalized soul is a contradiction in terms. It matters little if the whole world is gained if the soul is lost. This single insight of Jesus justifies all the Christian scriptures. The value of interior development is incomparably greater than all the information and acquisitions available through all the technologies of the present age. Without this consciousness, the metaphysically minded individual cannot sustain himself and must have recourse to the social or material props of the culture.

~ ~ ~

The development of personality in *Homo sapiens* is a metaphysical phenomenon of the first order, analogous in the physical world to the giant sequoia tree, the sperm whale, or the extinct mastodon. It is one of the great phenomena of life. There is no need for societal approval of a developed personality any more than a sequoia tree requires admirers to confirm its significance. The self intuits its own importance just as it intuits the lesser importance of the report of the senses with respect to the outer world. One can cast doubt on the report of the senses but every individual knows that they must be taken into account. How much more this is true for the interior self!

No single person can comprehend the entire metaphysical cosmos of which he is a part just as he cannot perceive the entire physical cosmos. His capacities do not reach that far. He can be certain of one thing, however, which is that the justification for his being does not derive from societal, family, national, or religious values. *It lies in the metaphysical reality in which he participates.* If this be mysticism, it is no more mystical than faith in the existence of the world of the senses. The trust in personal intuition is the foundation of metaphysical existence. It is a trust that one can count upon as being well founded.

TOWARD A RADICAL METAPHYSICS

The Need for Metaphysics—In all eras, metaphysical thought is the driving force of civilization. Today this force is largely unacknowledged. It is unacknowledged because the metaphysical will to development has no place in the paradigms of modern science. Yet all of the values, the aspirations, the ambitions, and compulsions that power societies have their basis in unacknowledged metaphysical phenomena underlying human activity. The tendency to neglect the metaphysical aspect of human life has always existed in the history of mankind but no era has so depreciated and disparaged metaphysics as the current one. Metaphysics is relegated to the realm of scholarly study or traditional religions where it exists in a tethered, tradition-bound form of little use to those seeking to develop their position in the universe. Parenthetically, it should be noted that the need for metaphysics is widely utilized by profit-seeking individuals who take advantage of the yearning for something more than the limited materialist approach to life.

One does not have to look far to discover the reason for the absence of influence of metaphysics in contemporary life. It can be found in the dogmas of modern science that have pervaded all aspects of our culture. Materialism is the foundation of life, any ideas lacking a material basis are regarded as lacking reality. Scientific study of the brain has replaced metaphysical study of the mind. If a concept is not based on weights or measures it is thrown out of court. These statements are not mere assertions; they represent the intellectual foundations of "developed" societies in the world today. In these societies, the media have grown to vast proportions, molding the tastes and values of the society to a degree previously unimaginable. Finally, the computer has become the central feature of modern life illustrating the powers and reach of technologically based science.

Today, any independent metaphysics is regarded as radical thinking, far removed from the mainstream of modern thought. However, in spite of the pervasive influence of the materialist dogmas, there is a *need for metaphysics,* to utilize a phrase from Ortega y Gasset (one of the last metaphysically minded philosophers of the twentieth century) that continually emerges in individuals with an independent mentality. Consciousness of the interior self is the principal factor developing the mind in a metaphysical direction. Scientific knowledge is of no value in this effort no matter how many studies of memory, language functions, or neuronal activity enter into the scientific literature. As for Christianity, the principal source of metaphysics in the western world, one may say its main virtue is that at least its ideas and values are metaphysical ones, albeit suited more for those with a limited intellectual conscience.

Paraphrasing Nietzsche's remark that there was only one Christian and he died on the cross, we may say that Søren Kierkegaard was the first and last absolute existentialist to achieve public recognition, albeit occurring long after his death. Existentialism merely means that an individual is committed to his metaphysical nature, i.e., his own feelings, thoughts, values, and desires, and gives them priority in his philosophical expression. Kierkegaard's repeated statement that "truth is subjectivity" contains the entire existential point of view and is far more meaningful than Sartre's more famous sophism "existence precedes essence." By 'truth,' of course, Kierkegaard does not mean two plus two is four or any form of factual knowledge but rather the scriptural concept that Jesus must have had in mind when he said, "I am the truth." Subjectivity is put forth as the supreme value in human life. One has to remember that the word "subjective" has pejorative implications in our culture indicating the vast divide separating the scientific mind-set from the metaphysical one. There is no great difficulty in grasping existential thought once one accepts the reality of the metaphysical self and the necessity for human beings to cultivate this aspect of their being.

"Truth is subjectivity" means that the essential feature in the life of an individual is his valuation of his interior self, i.e., his subjective self. There is no greater tragedy than the failure of an individual to realize this value. What hinders this development, however, is the modern view that there is no such thing as the self, that there is only a complex arrangement of synapses and neurons in the brain, giving rise to the illusion of self. Without a belief in the metaphysical self, humans are at the mercy of their environment, which in the present age cares little for the development of an interior self. Only a radical metaphysics will save the individual from drowning in the swamps of the materialist dogmas of contemporary society. There is a pressing necessity for metaphysics for any individual in today's world who has respect for himself as an independent being.

~ ~ ~

The Search for Reality—If there is a common denominator that the materialist viewpoint shares with the metaphysical one, it is to be found in the "search for reality." There is general agreement that reality is what is to be valued and illusion is to be avoided. Henry David Thoreau remarked that the instrument the world is in need of is a *realometer* that will locate reality. All agree that the truth refers to what is real; falsity indicates the presence of the unreal. If Kierkegaard claimed that truth (reality) is subjectivity, the entire world of science and technology has replied, "No, truth is objectivity." The real world is the objective world subject to measurement, analysis, and control. Whatever one's values and attitudes, it is the object world that in the end is what counts.

Where then is the real world really to be found? This is the burning issue confronting every individual, young or old, male or female, white-skinned or colored-skinned, Jew or Christian, free-thinker or traditionalist. Every self-respecting individual wants to participate in the real world. How is one to know where it is to be found? In the absence of a realometer, the individual has to make up his own mind as to its characteristics. For the vast majority of people, this decision is an unconscious one, framed by the culture and traditions in which their minds developed. In the "progressive" world of science, objectivity and material being represent the real world and the successful life consists in obtaining the maximum of *materia* and power available, utilizing the analytic objective techniques developed in western societies. Possession and utilization of *materia* represent participation in the real world. Tradition-bound societies have a different approach; for them, reality is to be found in one's connections with the members of one's family, race, or religion, and the successful life consists of strengthening and solidifying these bonds. This is a metaphysical attitude toward life since it emphasizes social continuity rather than material acquisitions. There is nothing concrete about one's relationships with those to whom he is connected by tradition or belief. The metaphysical self, however, is not emphasized; rather it is one's connections to the extended group that are valued above all else.

It needs to be recognized that the dichotomy between scientific and metaphysical is a false one because all values or conscious orientations inescapably have a metaphysical basis. No matter how objective or analytic one may be, his preferences in life are based on personality factors that do not have a material basis. One cannot demonstrate scientifically that the will to material success is a desirable or undesirable trait. One can analyze the consequences of this or that mental trait, one can perform correlations of outcomes with attitudes, one can theorize about the causes of human behavior *ad infinitum*, but in the end, the orientation of an individual is a *subjective* phenomenon, not to be explained by objective analysis. The distinction between various worldviews lies in the depths of the human mind. These distinctions are greatly affected by one's culture and upbringing, but ultimately turn out to hang upon the personal temperament and strength of mind of the individual. At all times and in all cultures there have been unregenerate materialists and unworldly metaphysicians. It should be remembered, however, that humans are deceptive creatures and materialists are prone to use metaphysics for very worldly purposes.

What I mean by radical metaphysics is a turning away from materialist or tradition-bound metaphysical values to an emphasis on the metaphysics of self—the one area where an individual can be certain his efforts will bear fruit. The metaphysical self is the domain of the individual, it is where his responsibility for development lies, it is the locale where he can be sure of his purposes. There is nothing really radical about concentrating on the development of self, it is the most natural and authentic arena for expression of one's energies. Kierkegaard's aphorism "Subjectivity is Truth" can serve as the slogan for an approach to the task of living, albeit minus his peculiar obsession with Christianity. The reality of the metaphysical self is a reality that transcends all others for the individual. *Materia* deteriorate and lose their value, communication is uncertain, love is the most untrustworthy of feelings, charity is usually misplaced. Social justice is almost always an illusion and societal power corrupts the individual. Only the realm of the metaphysical self offers a continuing source of fulfillment to the individual in search of the real world.

~ ~ ~

Reality of the Metaphysical Self—Again, all consciously willed human activity is founded on metaphysics. That is because willed activity is a function of values, of what one considers worth doing. Contemporary neuroscientists would have us believe that consciousness and free will (a corollary of consciousness) are illusions and that all purposeful activity is a function of prior conditioning or instinctive behavior. They reject the compelling intuition of individuals that they are the masters of their fate because this intuition does not fit the materialist dogmas about the brain. There is no place for consciousness and free will in networks of neurons.

Scientific materialists reject metaphysics. However, there are compelling reasons to reject the materialist point of view.

Physical investigations over the past century have made it clear that there is far more reason to reject the reality of perceived *materia* than there is to reject the reality of the metaphysical self. The objectivity of 'objects' has disappeared as particle physics has attempted to delve into their ultimate reality. Kant's original insight, stated in ponderous philosophical jargon, was that the perceptive apparatus of humans determines their view of the world. If he had paid more attention to the noumena and less to the phenomena, he would have been a greater philosopher. He muddied the waters of his insight by later attempting to conciliate church and state and pass judgment on matters outside his abilities. Nevertheless, more attention should be paid to his fundamental observation. The clarity of the intuition of the metaphysical self exceeds the subjectively determined perceptions of external *materia*. It should be recognized that this observation is not new in human intellectual history since it forms the basis of Hindu and Buddhist philosophy. "Atman is Brahman" can be equated with "Truth is Subjectivity."

It is not without reason, however, that the materialist dogma has become ensconced in the developed world and is well on the way to becoming established worldwide. The feeble efforts of popes and preachers and the not-so-feeble efforts of Muslim clerics and fanatics are clearly on the losing side of the battle with materialism. The materialist viewpoint has a *utilitarian* value that is of great consequence for the human psyche. Whereas consciousness of reality may not be much enhanced by science, technology, and the consumerism associated with them, they bring an enormous power to dominate nature.

Relative security is provided to individuals with access to this power. Human beings are attracted to it as bees are by honey. It is not merely a matter of material or monetary acquisitions but also of the prestige and influence associated with technical capacities. The world loves a conqueror, which is what the modern captain of industry or science represents. Nietzsche's recognition of this aspect of human psychology led him to postulate the "will to power" as the driving force of human affairs.

~ ~ ~

The Will to Self-Development—It is very natural for individuals to endeavor to provide for their security, to prolong their life, to look after their offspring, to obtain as many things as they can that make life more comfortable, more stimulating, and more interactional with others. Erotic fulfillment is one of the essential ingredients to the good life. Experiences and capacities of all kinds are sought after by individuals with a strong sense of self. All this is greatly enhanced by possession of material resources that can aid the individual in his quest for the good life. Money, the abstraction representing all material possessions in a developed society, becomes a central feature in the efforts of the individual to find satisfaction in life.

During the greater part of their life, most people lead an essentially automatic existence. They may appear to be functioning at a high level in society but the basis of their activities is determined by their culture, environment, and past experiences. In this sense, the behaviorists and neuroscientists are justified in rejecting the existence of a metaphysical consciousness. To this extent, the neuronal theory of the mind is sufficient to account for the human phenomenon and thus may be deemed to possess "truth", at least as much truth as the human is capable of ascertaining. However, there is more to the human phenomenon than stimulus-response activities, no matter how complex they may become.

Every individual capable of conceptualizing his own being intuits that there is an energy within him that lies outside of the categories mentioned above. This is the metaphysical self whose reality is more firmly based than the object world since it is known independently of our limited perceptual system. What to do with the metaphysical self is the great challenge of human life. To ignore it or regard it as something questionable and ancillary to the main business of material living is to ignore one's own inner reality, the one unforgivable sin in life. The fact that scientific dogmas do not recognize the metaphysical self is not pertinent since this is an area in which science and technology have nothing to contribute.

Along with the will to live and the will to power, which represent lower levels of functioning of the metaphysical self, one needs to recognize the will to self-development, representing the highest-level function of the metaphysical self. No technical apparatus is needed to perceive this feature, it is only necessary to examine one's own self and recognize the latent or not-so-latent need to go beyond the status quo. The person who does not recognize this need within himself is metaphysically comatose although he may appear quite alive in the external world. This need manifests itself in many ways: through learning, through religion, through creative endeavor of whatever sort. It can be suppressed through excessive engagement in societal activities that tempt one to neglect their inner selves. The art of life consists of discovering the route to metaphysical development. One thing is certain—

accumulation of wealth, power, or prestige will never lead to fulfillment in this area. Nor will doing good for others no matter how worthwhile this activity may appear. The self needs be developed in a metaphysical manner, which means personal growth and development. Attending to the needs of others, whether they be family, friends, or the underprivileged, is another matter with its own considerations but not relevant to the subject under discussion.

A question that needs to be faced in a discussion of the human will to self-development is why such a will should exist at all. Animals do not possess it although they clearly have a will to live and even manifest a will to power. Why do not humans rely on their instincts and cleverness at survival without troubling themselves about metaphysical self-development? The only absolutely legitimate answer to this question is that this is the way things are for human beings. Just as the will to live exists in living creatures without evident explanation, so the will to self-development exists in humans without explanation. This is the way we are. Biologists would have their audiences believe that self-development along with morality, ethics, and power drives are all manifestations of a basic will to live, if not solely for the individual than for his kindred and offspring. One is hard-pressed to see how this could be the case since the will to self-development is often contrary to survival, longevity, and family wellbeing. As an aside, it should be stated that recourse to erudite discussions about DNA replication and cellular programs explains nothing about the *reasons* behind the will to anything. They merely describe the mechanisms of biological existence that have evolved in the course of the development of life. They relate to a different category of existence.

Human beings have an insatiable need to know as part of their metaphysical nature. Aristotle felt this need to be the principal characteristic of thinking humans. Of all the things humans would like to know about, the principal one is the meaning of their existence. If no plausible ideas are available, the thinking person will conclude that this is an absurd world with absurdity as the dominant feature of human activity. In the *Phaedo*, Socrates relates his vision of an afterlife in which evil (ignorance) is punished and good (self-development) is rewarded. He admits, however, that his vision is an approximation that should not be expected to be correct in every detail. But he stood behind the essential message and counseled his followers not to despair about his immanent death. Similarly, envisioning the purpose of self-development requires a metaphysical orientation since there can be no biological (i.e., materialist) answer. Since the metaphysical sense of self has a firmer basis in reality than does the materialist outlook, we are entitled to look to it for understanding the phenomena of the will. Let us say that while the process of self-development occurs in a time-bound dimension, its *consequences* lie outside of the time dimension and are eternal. Every developed human represents a point of metaphysical light in the universe. Every developed human participates in the creation of this universe as if he were a part of a vast pointillist canvas, which is the metaphysical cosmos. This canvas does not have spatial or temporal dimensions but has its own dimensions that are metaphysical in nature. Therefore, it behooves every intelligent being to deliver the maximum possible energy to his light in this life so that he will play his proper part in the canvas of which he is a part.

Like Socrates, I do not expect this metaphor to absolutely mirror the reality of metaphysical existence. No metaphor can accomplish this task. But something like it must be true. If one does not intuit this purpose to human life, then he will necessarily fall back upon the feeling that he lives in an absurd world with all the nihilistic and cynical consequences implicit in a worldview founded on absurdity.

~ ~ ~

The Dimension of Time—"Time is the river I go afishing in" was the comment of Henry David Thoreau who brought his laconic Yankee wit to bear on the subject. Thoreau was prone to Heraclitean-like aphorisms, suggesting great depth but hard to decipher. For philosophers, time is indeed a very mysterious concept. Many of the most important thinkers of the past century have attempted to decipher this mystery. One can mention Bergson, Berdyaev, Husserl, Heidegger, and Ortega y Gasset. Consideration of the phenomenon of time dates back to Augustine whose analysis remains one of the most profound. No discussion of time can afford not to mention Kant and Einstein who underlined the relationship of the time dimension to the human observer, albeit from vastly different perspectives.

Most western thinking views time as a linear phenomenon analogous to a straight line in space. Time is unalterable, measurable, and continuously progressing forward. However, there are other ways of viewing the phenomenon of time. Cyclical time is based on the concept that all events are repetitive and better represented by a circle rather than a line. Eastern and Mesoamerican civilizations believed in the cyclical nature of time, which is supported by the cycles characterizing events occurring in the heavens as well as on our planet earth. Finally there is the concept of "existential time" as a single point. This idea was developed at length by Nicolai Berdyaev, which emphasized the present moment as the only form of time having metaphysical significance for the individual. Conversely, Henri Bergson considered "the moment" to be of no consequence since time is a continuous function expressing the ceaseless changes that characterize reality.

Bergson's view is more congruent with the real world. There is no such thing as "the present" available to the conscious mind, there is only the past in the process of becoming. The future is an imaginary concept indicating the plans, calculations, anticipations, and desires of the metaphysical self. None of them may ever occur. However, the visions of the future are an indication that the past may be enlarged. Properly speaking, the future does not belong to the category of time but is an imaginary human mental construct.

What we are as individuals is all in the past, our consciousness of self and the world is all of past events. What is referred to as "the present" is merely the immediate past that has just been created. The past is what is meaningful to a thinking person, it is what he has made of himself and what he has to show for the enormous effort required by life. Living in the past is all that is available to the conscious mind. This should be enough to satisfy the cravings of the most demanding of individuals.

The present is a virtual concept like that of the infinite divisibility of a line or the beginning of time or the end of space. It refers to the position of the self at an infinitesimal point in time. When a person thinks he is living in the present, experiencing life and enjoying himself, it only means that he is pleased with the recent past he has just created. It may be sensations, stimuli, or accomplishments that he has just added to his past which please him. Enjoyment of the present means satisfaction with the immediate events of the past. One's memory may be exceedingly vivid of the events of the immediate past but they are still the past and cannot be rescinded. The main distinction to be made of one's time preferences is whether the recent past or remote past is of greater interest to the individual. However, the direction of one's life requires a proper consideration of the entire range of the past that the individual has created. Free will is dependent on awareness of the past.

It is difficult to conceive of time except from a metaphysical perspective. Appreciation and utilization of the past requires an awareness that the past has not disappeared but has taken its place in the temporal continuum of metaphysical existence. This awareness is the outcome of inner development since it is not customary to realize the permanent existence of past events. Animal nature has no capacity for this awareness. Memory in animals, including the human animal, originally was meant to avoid dangers and facilitate gratifications. When a human being comes to apprehend the permanence of the past, animal nature is transcended.

Unlike modern word processors, there is no erasing the writing of the metaphysical self. One's past is created for all eternity. Great care needs to be taken with life, as its record is permanent. This is a frightening thought but one that needs to be assimilated. Yet people allow their lives to be heedlessly spun out as a function of their instincts, habits, and early upbringing. It is not an "immortal soul' that a person needs to concern himself about, it is the life that is the eternal and irrevocable record of his existence.

Angst emerges when the metaphysical self is dissatisfied with the life it has created. Yet judgments of the past that has been created are an essential part of the continuing process of formation of a human life. Without judgments on the past, the metaphysical self has an insufficient basis for the exercise of its free will. Living in the future means planning for the past. Only death ends this process for the individual. Then "the moving finger stops and writes no more."

Genesis tells us that God created the world and saw that it was good. Like so many biblical legends, the creation myth embodies a fundamental reality, which is the judgment that human beings pass on their own created lives. It should be remembered that God did not remain satisfied with what he created—Nietzsche joked that his death was due to his grief over the human race—nor do humans remain satisfied with their own creations. We are not told if God felt Angst on observing the early behavior of his products but such may have been the case if He is truly the ground of all being.

The instruments that measure time inexorably beat out the moments, apparently for all eternity. Time, like space, seems to go on forever. Yet it is as impossible to imagine endless time as it is to imagine an end to time. Kant pointed this out in one of his antinomies. The whole idea of linear time is bound up with memory, which facilitates life's activities. Absent human beings, linear time would not exist, there would only be objects participating in the cycles of the universe. Time is a relative dimension analogous to space and completely dependent on human perception.

Perhaps the most important feature of linear time for an individual is the event of death. This event signifies that life—a metaphysical phenomenon—no longer animates a physical body. Isolated cells and organs may remain viable for a period of time but the phenomenon of organismic life has been terminated. In a human being, the metaphysical self, which is life rising to the level of consciousness, no longer manifests itself. The question of what happens to this metaphysical "energy" is a mystery not resolvable through the use of laboratory instruments. The creative energy returns to the mysterious source from whence it arose. Death is a metaphysical event and can only be envisioned in metaphysical terms.

The idea that one's soul, i.e., the metaphysical self, can be immortal is a useless concept in spite of long religious tradition. First of all, no one will ever know if his soul is immortal in a linear time frame. Secondly, what the individual cherishes is his life on earth, not an ethereal existence in some questionable beyond. The real significance of the idea of immortality is connected to the fear of punishment for one's sins. This is why discussions of hell are so much more vivid then those of heaven. The fear of consignment to hell has been historically far more significant then the dubious pleasures of paradise. With the advance of science, the concept of immortality has receded for the most part into the domain of religious superstition. There is no place for an immortal soul in the universe mapped out by astronomers. Rather one should envision that death marks out the temporal limits of his existence. It does not mean non-existence any more than passing beyond the spatial limits of an individual means that he is non-existent. The life of a person occupies its own niche in a metaphysical reality that death does not abolish.

One thing stands out saliently—the essential significance of a human life lies in the fact of its own existence and not in its presumed effects within societal structures. Families, societies, and nations are social constructs, not metaphysical ones. They ultimately exist to serve the metaphysical reality of the individual. Judgments of history do not alter this reality. The importance given to the individual by litterateurs or historians, usually in a self-serving context, has little meaning in the larger scheme of things. Kierkegaard was just as important in his lifetime as he was a century later after his discovery by philosophers and theologians. The fact that one has existed within a specified time interval and has possessed consciousness amidst a repertoire of capacities, feelings, and experiences is reason enough to be satisfied with life. There are no other satisfactions grounded in reality.

~ ~ ~

Values—The existence of "values" is the single most persuasive piece of evidence that human beings are part of a larger metaphysical reality. Values represent the feeling that there is something more to life than survival and procreation. There is nothing in the materialist view of human life that can explain the depth and diversity of human values. The search for meaningful values may be regarded as the great "existential" duty of the individual. Failure to perform this search means that the individual has abdicated his responsibility to make something more of himself than existed at the time of his birth.

Acceptance of the values handed to one by his society and culture indicates abdication of this responsibility. It requires no effort to follow patterns laid down by others in conducting one's life. It requires great effort to develop one's own values when they are contrary to those of family or society. In the materialist culture of today, the pressures to adapt materialist values are overwhelming. It is tragic to see young people be exclusively educated toward a trade instead of toward enlarging their personal horizons. It is tragic when the pressures of family dictate the direction of one's life instead of finding a direction for enlarging the metaphysical self. It is tragic to see the temptations of power and prestige override the need to establish one's own interior self.

The metaphysical self does not automatically come into existence without an effort of will. One needs to struggle and endure in order for this event to occur. Nor is there any end to creating the metaphysical self; there is only the end of biological life when the opportunities to perform this feat are terminated. Valuation of this accomplishment is essential for it to occur. *Purity of heart is to will one thing* is the title of a famous essay by Kierkegaard. The one thing that needs to be willed is creation of the metaphysical self. However, if there is no belief in its existence, it will never come to pass. The crime of those who espouse the worldview of science and technology is to have undermined the individual's intuition of his metaphysical self.

Belief in the metaphysical self is the most natural thing in the world for an individual; however, the scientific dogmas of the times have persuaded many that it does not exist. Materialist thought has overwhelmed the intuition of a nonmaterial self, which is regarded as an intellectually puerile idea. Most value their bank account more than their soul. There are consequences to this perversion of human values, the principal one of which is the loss of the metaphysical self. An individual who has not developed this essential feature of his life appears superficial, unaware, without depth to his or her personality. They are, at bottom, like children, dependent on the crutches of society and lacking mental depth. Generosity, friendliness, liveliness, family relationships, or a clever mind do not make up for this lack. There is a certain sadness engendered when one sees how many people reach old age without the depth of thought that can only come from the development of a metaphysical self.

~ ~ ~

Self-development and Egoism—The principal requirement for the development of a metaphysical self is the emergence of the prior consciousness that all in the world of senses is not as it seems to be. It is a consciousness that generates awareness of self as something more than a stimulus-response entity. How this consciousness emerges in a flesh and blood person is a great mystery. The Christian concept of a "state of grace" is as good an explanation as any, but answers the question of how grace is dispensed with the facile but meaningless resort to "God's will", a concept largely devoid of meaning in the modern world. Those with a metaphysical consciousness, however, are in a state of grace by whatever means this may occur.

Concentration on self without a metaphysical consciousness leads to a crude egotism that is justly condemned in civilized societies. No matter how well-meaning an individual may be, self-centered activities without metaphysics is a road to personal disaster. Narcissism, greed, acquisitiveness, ingratitude, and insensitivity are the personality features of the individual who centers on his own self in the absence of awareness of a metaphysical dimension in his existence. The term "selfish" is universally looked upon as a damning

57

condemnation of an individual because of the prevalence of self-centeredness without metaphysics. It is an unfortunate truth that charitable activities and preoccupation with "helping" others in no way eliminates selfishness.

The consciousness of a metaphysical self facilitates the participation of the social self in societal affairs without the need for inordinate power and prestige. One can more readily fulfill the requirements of the social compact when it is clearly distinguished from fulfilling the metaphysical self. Obligations self-incurred such as the raising of children or payment of debts are naturally fulfilled when one has a sense of self not limited to social circumstances. On the other hand, obligations not self-incurred such as demands of family, religion, or society can be weighed against the needs of the metaphysical self. The individual did not ask to be born into a specific set of circumstances and has every right to change them regardless of the expectations of others. One should not be expected to conform to life-long vows entered into on the basis of societal traditions.

The question of how one develops and strengthens the metaphysical self has as many answers as there are people with a metaphysical consciousness. Every individual must look to himself for the answer. There are obvious general categories increasing consciousness such as education, acculturation, creative activities, significant experiences, acquisition of capacities, and so forth. It is frequently not recognized that the experiences of war, illness, or prison, whatever their disadvantages, often lead to metaphysical development. The mind that one brings to these categories is more important than their specific nature. Ultimately, a metaphysical cosmovision emerges that greatly strengthens one's position in life.

The person who seeks to develop his metaphysical self in modern society appears to be a radical personality once his true orientation is known. He usually finds himself uncomfortable in meaningful discussions with others since his orientation is different from most other individuals. Metaphysics leads to a value system radically divergent from those held by others in a society dominated by capitalist, Christian, and scientific-technological influences. Radical metaphysics, however, is a necessity for personal development. Those without it remain partially developed people who do not fully realize their human potential.

~ ~ ~

The Question of God—One cannot discuss metaphysical beliefs in the context of a western orientation to culture without coming up against the concept of God. The most significant metaphysical expressions in this culture exist within a religious framework. Christianity is essentially metaphysics superimposed upon Judaic religion. The concept of spirit was developed by apostles and church fathers with copious borrowings from Plato and Aristotle. However, for the Greeks after Socrates, metaphysics was a scholarly activity, whereas spirituality (i.e., metaphysics) was life itself for the early Christians. Later most of the significant ideas about metaphysics came from the Christian priesthood until the rise of secular universities in Europe. Virtually all major existentialist writers, with the notable exceptions of Nietzsche and Sartre, have included something like the idea of God in their worldview, whether this idea was mystical or intellectual in origin. No one expressing himself with a metaphysical orientation can long avoid the subject of God even if it be in order to reject it.

59

The most important thing to be said about the belief in God is that it is usually based upon one's upbringing or early influences from family and society. The belief represents an indoctrination foisted upon one during childhood when its evaluation is not possible. Belief in God stemming from childhood indoctrination is merely parroting noises in the environment and has little more significance than a parrot's ability to mimic the sounds heard by it in its cage. The fact that feelings of piety and reverence can be engendered by early exposure to church music, chants, awe-inspiring cathedrals, or eloquent preachers only means that it is human nature to have these feelings, but is most certainly not reason to believe that God exists. Brain washing is not a reputable means to induce metaphysical intuitions. Nor does the fact that belief in God has antecedents going back thousands of years and is found in most cultures provide any more persuasive evidence. Most men believed the earth was flat thousands of years and that witches could put hexes on them for at least as long but these ideas have turned out not to be true. A metaphysically significant belief in God has to come from other sources.

Beginning with Aristotle and proceeding through the scholastic philosophers of the Middle Ages right through and including Spinoza (who was similar in temperament to the intellectuals of the church albeit originating from a different tradition), philosophers endeavored to prove the existence of God by intellectual means. The cosmological proof of God, the ontological proof, and other mental gyrations, especially the torturous mathematical proofs of "God" offered by Spinoza, were regarded as evidence that his existence was demonstrable by rational means. Fortunately, these ideas have been largely consigned to the dustbin of intellectual history. Kant is the principal figure responsible for this great advance and should be regarded as the equal of Copernicus or Newton in providing western intellectual culture with a liberating instrument. It is clear today that one cannot rationalize himself into a belief in God.

How then can one come to a belief in God? Belief in a metaphysical concept like God can only come from metaphysical experiences or intuitions that reveal His presence. This is the only route to theology that does not violate one's intellectual conscience. The authentic existentialistic thinkers, beginning with Kierkegaard, who professed a belief in God, testified that they came to it by this means. There is no alternative to a mystical sense that He exists. Either one has had this experience or has not. There is no middle ground. There is no defining the concept of God nor is there any means of delineating his activities. Any effort in this direction is crass superstition. There are those who have claimed that religious symbols have value in bringing one to the knowledge of God but this is a primrose path to spiritual obtuseness or worse. If one does not experience God directly, he has no basis for believing in him. Mystical experience is necessary. While some "mystical" experiences are undoubtedly delusional in nature, this does not mean all can be placed in this category. The fact that some merchants are dishonest does not mean all are thieves. Genuine personal experiences of God must be recognized as a possibility of the human condition.

Having said this, the fact remains that few people today claim to have had direct experiences of God. The prolific biblical accounts of visions and experiences of God or of his human form as Jesus Christ seem to come from another universe, sharing nothing in common with the world of today. Most prayers directed to God serve the purpose of trying to extricate oneself from difficult situations or obtaining something that is greatly wanted. It is sad but true that all the reasons one would like to believe in God must be sacrificed on the altar of reality. None of them would pass the test of Thoreau's realometer. God as the opiate of the people degrades the human condition and God as the metaphysics of the masses is barely an improvement. It is necessary to make one's way in this vale of tears called civilization without the comfort of belief in a divinity, especially one that has the interests of the believer in mind. A metaphysical orientation, for most individuals, must do without the concept of God.

~ ~ ~

Yearning for the Transcendent—Relinquishing the idea of God does not mean that one need relinquish an intuition of a transcendent reality. To a great extent, the popularity of the idea of God is dependent upon the presence of a yearning in the hearts of many to discover some form of a transcendent reality. The whole structure of eastern philosophy is based upon cultivation of this yearning. The significance of the transcendent in the human condition is far more evident in Buddhism and Brahmanism than in the western religions.

What does it mean to yearn for the transcendent? First and foremost, it implies a metaphysical consciousness in which the yearning can exist. The sum total of life's experiences leads those with a receptive mind to become aware that all is not as it seems and there is an underlying common reality shared by living, thinking beings. This proposition was first stated by Heraclitus millennia ago in a manner that has never been quite equaled in forcefulness of presentation. In this reality, the individual with his intuitions and ideas looms large as opposed to his insignificance amidst the concrete facts of a supposed "real" world. Heraclitus referred to this reality as the "logos", a thought that was utilized by the author of the gospel of John, and one that has served as a model for philosophers throughout the ages. The reality shared by all thinking beings is a *transcendent* reality based on the commonality of thought. It is not based on the physical world that exists only as a construct of the senses. It is impossible for a metaphysically minded individual to immerse himself in the thoughts and feelings expressed by similar individuals throughout the ages without sensing something connecting him with them. This intuition lends meaning to the idea of a transcendent reality connecting metaphysically aware individuals. The dimensions of time and space do not affect this reality, as it is a metaphysical phenomenon.

The transcendental movement in the United States emerging in the early part of the nineteenth century reflected the consciousness of shared metaphysical reality. Ralph Waldo Emerson was the outstanding leader of this movement. However, it was short-lived as a historical phenomenon since consciousness in the U.S.A. was to be largely shaped by the likes of Thomas Edison and Henry Ford rather than Emerson and Thoreau. Transcendentalism was relegated to odd personalities and finally disappeared as a significant philosophical movement. Materialism became the order of the day in the U.S.A., which it has continued to be up until the present time. The neglect of Emersonian ideas except as scholarly exercises has been a scandalous feature of American intellectual history. A rebirth of North American transcendentalism is long overdue.

~ ~ ~

Metaphysics—In one of Plato's dialogues, Socrates is made to say that Sophists can be recognized by the fact that they take money for their teachings. The ancient Greek sophists claimed to teach their students how to be successful in the world through acquisition of wisdom. The principal point was to be successful in society. In this sense, there was an honesty to their approach since it is undoubtedly possible to teach students how to be successful in the world of affairs.

However, it is certainly not possible to teach metaphysical reality by similar techniques. If there is one thing the existential movement in philosophy has made evident, it is that personal authenticity—the very essence of metaphysics—is not a matter to be taught through didactic means. The claim that metaphysical truths can be communicated for a fee is a contradiction in terms. Metaphysics requires self-development and self-development is not something that occurs in an instructional setting, much less one in which the 'student' has paid to attend. Metaphysical reality requires personal development, not classroom lessons. The only way to hope to directly teach metaphysical reality is by example through one's own personality and the ideas that are part of it. For the most part, the limited presentation of self to another does not bear metaphysical fruit and it is fraudulent to claim that it will—especially for pay.

The motives that impel an authentic metaphysically minded person to present his intuitions and thoughts to others have little to do with the edification of his hearers. Every creative person knows that the expression of himself through his own talents is a form of self-fulfillment, not a catering to the needs or wishes of others. Once he starts taking money for his expressions, he is on a road to marginalization of his creative self. He becomes a teacher instead of a metaphysical being. There are things that can be taught and should be taught, and it is appropriate to receive fees for these services. But the development of the metaphysical self is not included among these. Market metaphysics ought to be avoided like the plague by those who aspire to personal development.

To the argument that creative and metaphysically minded individuals must also earn their living, one can answer, yes, but not by selling fraudulent goods. St. Paul was a tent-maker, Spinoza an oculist, Nietzsche lived off his meager pension, and Kierkegaard inherited money from his father. When Kierkegaard ran out of money, he died. It is necessary for everyone to obtain a living; however, not through the sale of unsalable spiritual property. Like Socrates, one can identify the market metaphysician by what he requires to gain access to his thoughts. If one's personal aspirations are in the area of development of the metaphysical self, these modern-day sophists should be shunned.

~ ~ ~

Religious Institutions—Organized religions exist and flourish. It is not possible to ignore this fact. The predictions of the humanists and scientists of the nineteenth century that religions were passé and on their way out as a significant element in society have not turned out to be true. The violent assaults on religious structures by Kierkegaard, Marx, and Nietzsche have been rejected by society. Religions are flourishing as never before whether they be traditional Roman Catholicism, missionary Mormonism, or militant Islam. In the United States, there are more people with specific religious affiliations than at any time in its history. President Dwight Eisenhower, not exactly a fountainhead of metaphysical truth, said that he didn't care what religion people had as long as they had some religious beliefs and associations. Religion is acceptable, religion is required, religion is a part of the national fabric of most countries. Schopenhauer's statement, meant facetiously, that religion is the metaphysics of the people is more true now than in his own era. Metaphysics and religious belief are fused together in an apparently inseparable manner.

However, it is well to recall Kierkegaard's dictum that "the crowd is always wrong." The near universal valuation of religious belief may turn out to be a misplaced value. It is worth considering the possibility. First of all, one must admit that religion is a great consolation for many individuals in times of adversity. This is why Marx called it "the opiate [not metaphysics] of the people." Opiates have their value, and in the case of religion, this consoling value has been proven. Secondly, if religion is usually a second-hand metaphysics, at least it is some metaphysics. Without religion, many people would sink into the swamp of unrestrained materialism, urged on by a culture of consumerism and the endless 'miracles' of modern science. Religion is the only social force in the world today that brings the individual to some awareness of his own soul and the existence of transcendent realities. Perhaps more than its consolatory value, this ability of religion to bring people to awareness of their own soul is the reason for its universal presence in the world and its astonishing survival in a scientific-technological society.

Still, the crowd is usually wrong. The metaphysical dogmas of organized religions can act on the individual in a harmful manner. Acquiescence to religious doctrines of any type of institution impedes the development of one's consciousness of metaphysical reality, i.e., his own soul and the transcendent aspects of his existence. If one believes that Jesus was God, the Bible imparts His truths, and the doctors of the church have set forth these truths' nature and material consequences, the possibility of personal metaphysical development is remote. The *sine qua non* of authentic living, development of a mind of one's own, is blocked as far as metaphysics is concerned. This is even more true when there is indoctrination of immature minds at an early age. When all the answers come from outside, there is little opportunity to develop one's own thoughts. And independent thoughts, it should be stressed, are the very essence of the metaphysical self. Similarly, but not quite as clearly, it can be noted that the consolatory function of religion may not be in the best interest of the individual. If one believes that an expired loved one is living in heaven, there is not much incentive to come to a more serious resolution of this loss. Painful experiences are necessary for metaphysical development but this will not occur when simplistic Band-Aids are applied to the wound. As in everything else in human life, personal fulfillment comes from the struggle for personal development.

There are some valid reasons for associating oneself with churches. In the Middle Ages, they provided the only access to the great minds of history. For many years it was the only way to obtain an education for most people and modern-day parochial schools and seminaries often still provide a superior type of education. Monastic living still provides an escape from the soul-deadening effects of materialistic society. A price is paid, however, in the loss of personal freedom. For the best reasons to affiliate oneself

67

with an organized religion, one should look to the great minds of modern times. Nicolai Berdyaev, regarded as a "Christian" existentialist, said he joined the Orthodox (Russian) church because its liturgy was esthetically superior to all others and there were less professions of faith required of him compared to other Christian sects. Kierkegaard felt a loyalty to his dead father, refusing to break with the Danish Evangelical Church for many years because of this loyalty. Many other examples of valid reasons for participation in religious institutions can be found. The harmful effects of religion can be avoided by maintaining one's own intellectual conscience intact and looking toward one's own self for discovery of the metaphysical dimension in life.

~ ~ ~

The Concept of Angst—Angst is a German word that entered into the vocabulary of philosophy through the writings of Søren Kierkegaard. It cannot be simply translated as anxiety because it rather refers to an inner sense of ill-defined dread, unconnected to any external danger. Those plagued with Angst have great difficulties in identifying the cause of their state of ill being; the problem seems to be rooted in the depths of one's personality. It is a "worm in the heart" not lending itself to removal short of death. Freud attributed Angst to guilt over sexual events or feelings in early life, which explanation no longer seems plausible as the universal source of Angst. Kierkegaard himself thought Angst a sign of alienation from God but this explanation does not seem any more acceptable than the Freudian one. Angst is often notably absent in those who have little concern with their relationship to a deity.

Angst may be best translated as a chronic bad conscience, *La Mauvaise Conscience*, described by Vladimir Jankovsky in a famous essay of the 1930s bearing this title. What is the cause of a chronic bad conscience? Murder, rape, sexual aberrations, great crimes against innocents are possible explanations. But the reality is that the overwhelming majority of those who feel Angst are individuals who have not committed any type of societal infraction and seem quite normal members of their society. Nevertheless, "the worm in the heart" mentioned by Nietzsche is a ubiquitous phenomenon in the modern world. "Forgive me father, I have sinned" is a universal feeling in western society and one of the reasons for the long-standing success of the Catholic Church. It is highly unlikely that the sins recounted in the confessional are responsible for the Angst of the faithful. But forgiveness has a consoling value even if the sins confessed have a dubious relationship to the mental state of the confessee.

In this as in so many other matters, Nietzsche has had a profounder intuition than most about the cause of this malady. Nietzsche's "worm in the heart" (he does not use the term Angst in this context) is due to sins against the self in the form of choices of careers that are unfulfilling. If Nietzsche did not say, he should have said that any act preventing one from becoming what he is is a source of Angst for the lifetime of the individual. Choosing a wrong career too early is one of these sins but there are many others such as a bad marriage, a failure to acquire education, excessive parenting, acceptance of crushing family responsibilities, dissipation of the interior self through vices, antisocial acts that ruin a life. Others could be added to the list. The common denominator is the sin against the metaphysical self, resulting in a failure to become what one is capable of becoming. Such a failure may produce lifelong Angst.

Angst, however, like other forms of pain, has a redeeming aspect. Angst can *motivate* the individual to take steps that will remedy the situation. Angst is the motor that can drive the individual to do what is necessary to make something of himself. In this respect, an awareness of the metaphysical self is essential, because if one does not intuit himself as a metaphysical entity, he will not generate Angst when its development is impeded. The creative individual who cannot rest until he brings forth his creation may not recognize that it is in his creative activity that he forms his real self. Others find their fulfillment in various ways through the development of personal experiences and capacities. Engaging in whatever is genuinely meaningful to the individual will form his metaphysical self. A society that principally values acquisition of goods and profit-making activities will not encourage the individual to develop his inner self. Angst is the consequence in individuals capable of this emotion.

~ ~ ~

Thoughts on *Caritas*—When Jesus was asked what was the great commandment in the law, he answered that one must love God with all one's heart, all one's soul, and all one's mind. Almost as an afterthought Jesus added that one should love thy neighbor as thyself. Elsewhere he defines this love as doing to others as one would wish to be done to himself. This afterthought has become the principal ethical content of Christianity even to the extent that God himself has been defined as love, meaning brotherly love. Human beings have always had great difficulties with the injunction that one must love God more than all else. God is an abstraction that does not lend itself readily to the emotion of love. It is easier to love the Son of God, Jesus

Christ, as a surrogate figure with a human face. Easiest of all is to do good to others, apparently fulfilling the second commandment of the New Testament without becoming involved with personal emotions that are difficult to feign.

Doing good unto others is not exactly the same as loving them. In fact, a case could be made that doing good for people is strongly associated with the development of a certain sense of superiority that, in theory, is not very Christian. Nietzsche focused on this aspect of Christianity in his major opus on the subject, *Genealogy of Morals.* His point was that Christian charity was a form of asserting power over one's contemporaries. Nietzsche had an unfortunate predilection for hyperbole that reduced the influence of his writings. Nevertheless, in this work, as in all Nietzsche's writings, there is a hard core of truth requiring recognition.

It is essential to distinguish between the ethics involved in fulfilling the social compact of the society in which one lives and charitable doing good for others. Participation in the social compact is essential if a society is to survive and provide the necessary backdrop for individuals to flourish. Doing good as a personally motivated activity, however, is a different matter requiring close attention. There is every reason to seriously doubt the health of a society in which alms-giving and charitable activities are a part of the societal fabric. Perhaps Jesus would have done better by suppressing his afterthought and leaving the emphasis on the first and only great commandment that deals with a metaphysical issue.

The principal problem is that of how one knows what is needed to do genuine good for others. It is easy to find examples in one's own life of how adversity is the source of the self-development. To remove adversity from life is to remove the most potent stimulus to one's own interior and exterior development. It is hard enough to know what decisions are best for one's own self without trying to make similar decisions in the life of another. More often than not, efforts to do good for others result in the opposite effect—bad is done to them. A generous gesture is one thing but sustained interference in the lives of others usually does no good to the recipient and adversely affects the personality of the doer. One need only look at the world of church charities and government welfare programs to find evidence of the truth of this assertion. Attention needs to be paid to one's own personal condition; there is more than enough material for honest work there to satisfy the most energetic of individuals.

~ ~ ~

Creativity—The creative impulse is the continuation of the will to know discussed above. The desire of the individual to objectivize his apprehensions of existence is at the heart of the metaphysical self. For the developed human mind, it is never enough to have formed a vision of the reality in which he lives, he must express this vision in some objective form whether it be a work of art, a macro-concept of existence, or a micro-concept of some aspect of this reality. The philosopher Nicolai Berdyaev in his book, *The Meaning of the Creative Act,* expressed the view that the creative impulse was the core phenomenon of the human condition. The elucidation of the mechanics of material existence is only a small part of the capacity of humans to apprehend the real world and perhaps the least interesting part of it.

The human capacity to apprehend, the "logos" exemplified in the metaphysical structure of the human mind, seems to be able to be matched to the logos of existence. That this match is never absolute is the reason why *perspectivism* is the best philosophy to apply to human knowledge. Each individual, dispersed as he is throughout time and space, brings a unique perspective to bear upon reality. The perspectives of others are interesting to the developed mind because they continuously enlarge one's knowledge of the broad canvas of reality. A distinctive mark of the metaphysically undeveloped creature, human or otherwise, is a lack of interest in the perspectives of other individuals.

The creative impulse in its purest form, distinguished from contaminating motives of prestige, power, and monetary gain, is one of the great mysteries of the human condition. Why should artists, poets, and writers give over the greater part of their lives to their chosen form of expression when the likelihood of material recompense is usually remote? The philosopher Epicurus, whose name has come to symbolize the hedonistic element of life, created over 300 manuscripts, far outstripping other philosophers of the antique world. Most of his time was spent toiling over his writings rather than enjoying the pleasures of eating, drinking, and social intercourse. What inner force drove Epicurus and drives all other creative personalities in the world to *objectivize* their insights in the form of their creative work?

The answer to this question lies in the metaphysical nature of human beings. No mechanistic theory of life, no piling on of DNA structures, no theories of neuronal networks in the brain can account for the sustained force of the creative impulse. This impulse cannot be accounted for by physiological descriptions of life processes. The same may be said of all aspects of life but is most starkly evident in the phenomenon of human creativity. The metaphysical nature of a developed individual contains a force within him pushing him continuously to create new forms of being. To ignore this aspect of self for the sake of societal expectations is to sell one's birthright for a mess of pottage. When society suppresses the creative impulse of individuals, it becomes a corrupting influence leading to anthill existence rather than to the shining points of light composing the metaphysical universe.

~ ~ ~

An Existential Cosmovision—Dostoevsky wrote in one of his works that if a person does not have his own concept of life, others are sure to impose some concept upon him. Human beings need a concept by which to orient their life; if they do not generate their own, then they will borrow the prevailing societal concepts of how to live, of which there are usually no shortages. The core element of the metaphysical self lies in creating a personalized concept of life. Here is to be found the real fruit of this self— requiring experience, intelligence, and intuitive insights. This is not to say that one's *situation* does not influence one's concept of life. Nothing can develop within the interior self without stimulation from the exterior world. However, the concept of self that arises from these experiences is personalized, reflecting the activity of the metaphysical self. The important thing is not the situation but the reaction to it. For metaphysical development to occur, this reaction must be completely personalized.

Those who have not acquired a consciousness of themselves as a metaphysical being or who suppress this consciousness because of allegiance to the prevailing scientific materialism of the day can only have a limited sense of their being. Its essential feature, the central metaphysical self, is ignored. Consequently, their concept will be limited to the mundane and superficial values espoused by a materialist society with Christian-socialist overtones. The value of the family tends to be overemphasized, accumulation of wealth is a *sine qua non*, hedonistic pleasures are felt to be the key to the good life. The absence of a consciousness of the significance of the inner self distorts the way in which a person lives his life.

The key to a fulfilling concept of life lies in the consciousness and valuation of one's metaphysical self. This intuition is more important than the intuition of the senses in which a picture of the external world is presented. There is no reason to reject this intuition merely because the dogmas of materialist science label it as mysticism. The label is meaningless since all human values and consciousness can be so labeled. The awareness of the metaphysical self represents the essential knowledge of the individual, the *logos*, to which all other knowledge is subordinate. It can be said that consciousness of the significance of self is what leads to consciousness of the significance of an outer world.

The creation of a cosmovision involves the imaginative faculty since there is no way in which the individual can have a complete knowledge of the cosmos. Nevertheless, one can expect elements of truth to be found in most cosmovisions if they are based upon an existential apprehension of "the way things are," to borrow a phrase from Lucretius. An article of faith of an existential cosmovision must be based on the preeminence of the human individual over and above societal structures. To paraphrase a famous Gospel thought, society is made for man, not man for society. Neither is there a 'world spirit' capable of being known by finite human beings; there are only metaphysically minded individuals striving to develop themselves. If there is a God, he is to be found in the striving of these individuals to move themselves on to a higher form of being. The billions of individuals stretched out over time and space can be imagined to represent pointillistic points of light creating a huge canvas called the human reality. Every individual has his place in this canvas and contributes to it according to his metaphysical substance. Those who do not develop metaphysical substance are part of the background of infrahuman life. The vastness of the inanimate universe may be viewed as a kind of setting in which the human phenomenon has developed.

Once having existed, the metaphysical self has a significance for all time. Death does not erase this significance, it merely places a period after it. In spite of the emphasis placed by our society on the interactional features of living, the metaphysical self is not required to have an obvious impact on societal structures or to directly affect other individuals. It is a significant phenomenon in its own right. The stars above do not require human observation to establish their significance in the scheme of things. The great works of nature are phenomena in their own right; they do not need humans in order to become important. They are part of a pattern of cosmic being of which *Homo sapiens* is the leading representative. We limited humans may not appreciate the significance of individual life phenomena or even the phenomenon of our own metaphysical selves but this should not be surprising. As Shakespeare noted, there are things in heaven and on earth beyond our puny abilities to understand. It is enough to intuit their importance.

All this may well be imaginative but can also be expected to contain elements of truth. It is the writer's personal cosmovision. As a concept of life, it has served him well. No doubt much modification and elaboration are possible, but its essential feature pertaining to the reality and significance of the metaphysical self will remain.

~ ~ ~

Genesis of an Independent Philosopher— Autobiographical notes have the principal value of helping a writer develop his own self-awareness—an essential element of the repertoire of every philosophically minded individual. Additionally, such notes can aid a reader to assess the writings into which he has chosen to delve. These are the two important reasons why one who writes a philosophical work should create a picture of his own personal development to supplement the statement of his thoughts. Every philosophy is set forth from and should be evaluated through the unique perspectives of the writer. Knowing something about the history of the writer is required for this evaluation. These notes have to do with what concerned my interior development; they are not meant to be a chronology of my life nor do they contain any details of my relationships. These are not relevant to the purpose at hand. I have revealed my life in greater detail in my book, *Behold The Philosopher* (2007).

I grew up in the New York City of the thirties and forties of the last century—a time of great social ferment in the life of the city. All four of my grandparents were Jewish immigrants from Czarist Russia. They all had very different personalities, but a common denominator in their outlook was a determination to assimilate into the culture of the United States. None would speak Yiddish, their native language, in my presence. My paternal grandmother of whom I have the fondest memories was illiterate. Nevertheless, she struggled mightily to make possible a professional education for all her three children. My father, the eldest, attended George Washington University medical school but was forced to drop out because of problems with his grades. He never spoke of this painful experience to me but I gradually became aware of the enormous impact it had on my life.

My inclination toward philosophy became evident during my early school years. I devoured all of the volumes of Will Durant on the history of thought at a time when my classmates were reading comic books and pornographic literature. On my own, I tried to master Latin, an effort that was not notably successful even though I spent many hours on the subject. High school is a dim blur in my mind but one thing I do remember was my pleasure in reading Voltaire in his native language as part of my course in French literature. There was little doubt where my interests lay during this period of my life. However, another set of influences was brought to bear on me that profoundly affected the direction of my life.

My father who had become a secondary school science teacher and my uncle who was a bacteriologist undertook together a sustained campaign to direct me toward medical school. I was sent to "work" in my uncle's laboratory, I was given a "project" in science to develop which culminated in a Westinghouse science prize, and I was led to view entry into medical school as the ticket to success in life. By the time I entered New York University as an undergraduate, the program for my life had become fixed without my ever squarely confronting the decision myself. Perhaps a certain character defect is present in my personality that allowed me to be influenced against my own inclinations.

Initially I was able to reconcile these opposing influences by majoring in philosophy while simultaneously registering in the premedical program. I took most of my philosophy with one professor, Dr. Harman Chapman, whose teaching style greatly appealed to me. He introduced me to the world of philosophical writings beginning with the ancient Greeks down to the existentialist movement in Paris that was flourishing at the time. But, of course, the moment came when a choice had to be made. Not only did my family influences lie heavily upon me, but I won a State Regents scholarship to attend medical school. It was all too much for me to resist at the age of nineteen years. I will never forget entering into the office of Dr. Chapman to tell him of my plans. He seemed disappointed when he learned I would be entering medical school. "Ah, so many are entering the field of medical sciences" was his only comment. At that moment, a worm entered my heart that was never to completely leave me.

The rest followed in a predictable manner. I established a career in academic neurology, which seemed to me the closest I could get to philosophy in my work but which, of course, was a completely unrealistic idea. I married, raised a family, and became a tenured university professor. However, the worm never left my heart. The contradictions within my psyche gradually grew more intense until at the age of fifty years I completely threw over the life I had constructed. I resigned my professorship, departed from my family—my children had become adults—and went to the San Francisco Bay area with the woman who was to become my permanent partner in life.

Once freed of my onerous career and finally finished with the role of paterfamilias, I plunged into a frenzy of creative writing. Poetry, novels, essays poured forth from my typewriter like lava from a long extinct volcano. But finally, my compass settled on a particular direction, the writing of philosophy. Almost every year some philosophical work emerged from my study—*Affirmations of Reality, Philosophical Artwork, Fanatic of the Mind, Souls Exist,* and *Reverence for the Soul.* There was a time when I devoted myself to aphoristic writings—*A Contemporary Logos, Sententiae, Sentences in Spaces.* All these were published at my own expense. I even dabbled in artwork, displaying my aphorisms in graphic form and exhibiting them at various locales. The one scholarly study I undertook, *The Legend of Nietzsche's Syphilis,* which drew upon my medical background, was published commercially underlining the fact that my own philosophical writings had no appeal for publishers.

None of this orgy of creativity was accompanied by any recognition in the world of literature, philosophy, or the arts. But I did not care—and still do not care—for it was enough for me to be able to express myself freely in whatever format I chose. I knew that becoming an independent philosopher at age fifty would not be the same as entering the field of philosophy at age twenty via graduate studies, acquisition of a Ph.D., positions in university departments of philosophy, and so forth. I was not to have the professional stimulation and critiques that were associated with a university career in philosophy. On the other hand, I was free to make of myself what I could, given access to libraries and having the time to develop my thoughts. I was aware of the opinions of Schopenhauer and Nietzsche about philosophy at the universities and I did not wish to contaminate my newfound freedom with the burdens of academic life. Even more relevant, perhaps, was the fact that the analytic orientation and anti-metaphysical bias of post-World War II American philosophy ran directly counter to my own convictions about the nature of philosophical thought.

Anyone who cares to examine my writings will find that throughout they have been affected by my "situation" as an independent philosopher. Similarly, they reveal the truth of Nietzsche's dictum that all philosophy reflects the temperament of the philosopher. Objective philosophy is an illusion not to be found in this world. I can say, however, that my work does not stem from the more mundane considerations of publication requirements for promotion or the income derived from writing university textbooks. The scathing essay of Schopenhauer entitled *Philosophy at the Universities* seems to me to be truer today than it was in his time.

On occasion, I have regretted my youth lost to the utilitarian considerations of an academic medical career. I wondered what would have happened if I had had a stronger sense of myself at age twenty and gone to postwar Paris to immerse myself in the whirlpool of existential thought. I might have floundered and come to nothing—or to something more than I am now. One never knows what would have been at the end of the road not taken. Nevertheless, I have made something of myself, albeit as a late bloomer in the domain of philosophical thought. I have been forced to come to grips with what I am. No doubt a benevolent providence has looked after me since now, entering the eighth decade of my life, I can truly state that I am content with the outcome of my life.

THE WILL TO METAPHYSICAL EXISTENCE

At the core of all human effort lies the will. Every ambitious executive, every earnest householder, every searching scientist, even those claiming to unlock the mysteries of the brain in materialist terms, are dependent upon their will in order to advance their projects. It is fashionable today to think all human activity to be a function of complex stimulus-response phenomena occurring within the confines of a computer-like brain. The modern scientifically-minded intellectual has persuaded himself that the soul—or whatever other term one prefers for the inner self—is merely an epiphenomenon of the firing of neuronal circuitry, which is the real cause of thought and behavior. The materialist society that has evolved in the present era has little use for the metaphysical concepts like the will or the soul.

However, the human will is not to be defined in materialist terms and is manifestly a metaphysical entity. It is an aspect of the metaphysical self. It is the arbitrator of all human activity, determining the ultimate direction of the individual. No form of society that ignores the will, i.e., the needs, desires, and aspirations of individuals, can hope in the long run to retain the allegiance of its members. Societies that deny opportunities for self-development ultimately give way to other forms of social arrangements.

The concept of democracy has captured the imagination of the civilized world because it promises spiritual freedom and material wellbeing to those living under its rule. Even if it has not always lived up to its promises, the ideal remains a powerful force that has overcome the competing ideals of communism and fascism.

Coincident with the ascendancy of the democratic ideal, there has arisen the unique proliferation of scientific technology that has been the engine responsible for the material prosperity promised by this ideal. A long and healthy life, substantial and spacious shelter, and the acquisition of innumerable material goods are possible only through the development of technologies that can provide them. People expect these things as a result of the expansion of democratic ideals. In the United States, the promise of a chicken in every pot has been expanded to include expectation of life-long economic security, permanent access to the miracles of modern medicine, computers and television sets in every household, and higher education for all children. These goals are becoming those of the entire planet following the example of American culture. It is no wonder that scientific technology is worshipped as the centerpiece of modern civilization, because without it all of the aspirations noted above would become only hopeless pipe dreams.

It is necessary to pay some attention to the glorification of scientific technology above and beyond valuing the products that flow from it. There is an underlying assumption that has become associated with scientific and technological activity. This is the assumption of *materialist monism*, i.e., that all existence is understandable through material phenomena that obey the laws of nature. What one can see, feel, hear, touch, and smell is what exists and nothing more. Material being is all there is, including our own selves, which is discernable through the senses albeit fortified by the enormous panoply of scientific instrumentation. Monistic belief is the *sine qua non* of the modern technological society. Religious dogmas carrying over from earlier views of the universe still exist but occupy an increasingly unimportant role in society. It is technical competence, not religious fervor, which determines the success of an individual in the democratic state.

It is still true, however, that the viability of a concept of life is dependent on the degree to which it corresponds with reality. If it is 'will' which underlies all human activity, then a concept of how to live life must be in accord with the properties of this animating will. It is remarkable how mundane are the concepts which deal with the human will compared to the complexity and sophistication of modern thought about the material universe and the history of humanity. No doubt this is because the concept of will is a *metaphysical* idea not subject to materialist investigation. For this reason, there is a discomfort and even disbelief regarding the will even though every reflective human being intuits within himself the existence of this will. Where scientific monism reigns, it is easier to regard the will as an illusory resultant of various stimuli that rarely reach the level of consciousness. That there may be an *existent* will, which is non-material in nature, is not an acceptable idea. This attitude has had far-reaching consequences for societies oriented to scientific technology.

~ ~ ~

The name of Arthur Schopenhauer is properly linked to the concept of will as the core of the human condition. His major work entitled *The World as Will and Representation* is the benchmark effort delineating will as the reality underlying existence, both animate and inanimate. Schopenhauer extended the concept of will far beyond its ordinary meaning, essentially equating it with all manifestations of the forces of nature. But his principal interest was in the human will, which he maintained was the central aspect of the self. Schopenhauer's will was a metaphysical idea, accounting for the disappearance of interest in his work in contemporary philosophy. His principal idea, however, is deeply insightful and deserving of study. Schopenhauer was also a monist but his monism was founded on his belief that 'will' represented the inner reality of all things. He was highly contemptuous of the metaphysical narrowness of the physics of his times, a situation that has changed little up to the present day.

Schopenhauer was a cynic and a pessimist who molded his philosophy to be in accord with his temperament. He did not *value* the human will and finally reached the point where he believed that the ultimate purpose of will was to cease willing. With this thought, his ideas approached eastern philosophies and can only be distinguished from Buddhist tracts by Schopenhauer's caustic wit. He became a peculiar hybrid incorporating a Voltairian bitterness into Buddhist resignation. All this, however, does not detract from the profundity of his original insight into the nature of the human condition.

He conceived all life to be animated by a metaphysical "will to live" which he easily correlated with the nineteenth century development of ideas about biological instincts. Humans were no different than other forms of life in the dominance of the will to live; they were only different in the complexity of the manifestations of this will. He was strikingly modern in his concept of consciousness as merely an evolutionary development to enhance the effectiveness of the will to live. However, he did concede that *Homo sapiens* manifested a will to knowledge that went beyond the will to live and ultimately could liberate an individual from the tyranny of this instinct. Here too, Schopenhauer's ideas are close to Buddhist teaching.

Friedrich Nietzsche, the most radical thinker of modern times, considered himself to be a disciple of Schopenhauer during his early years. Later, after he rejected many of Schopenhauer's ideas, observing that all philosophies expressed the temperament of their authors, a thought that is equally applicable to both himself and Schopenhauer. Nietzsche tried to modify his predecessor's doctrine through his concept of a will to power that he thought more accurately defined the nature of the human will. Nietzsche prepared extensive notes on this subject but never could bring his ideas to fruition in a completed writing. It may be that he was never satisfied with the idea. After his death, his sister published his notes following her own ideas about his philosophy, which, however, were far removed from Nietzsche's views. The concept of a "will to power" was to have far-reaching influence on German politics in the first half of the twentieth century. Today, at the beginning of the twenty-first century, considerations about the "will" are of interest only to scholars whose business it is to study the history of psychology and philosophy. To borrow a phrase from Nietzsche, the concept is now thoroughly "untimely" (*unzeitgemässe*). It is necessary to consider the question as to why, in the present age, one should sift through the ashes of a discarded nineteenth century concept. This question turns on the meaning of philosophy itself, the question of why anyone other than scholars should turn to philosophy at all.

~ ~ ~

The "desire to know," identified by Aristotle as the principal feature of human existence, dominates the individual from his earliest beginnings in life until his vital energies flag towards its ending. Curiosity to explore his world marks the child's first efforts as an independent person. Later this desire (i.e., will) manifests itself in diverse ways through the many avenues of personal experience available in modern society. At the root of it all is the will to experience the world, which is merely another way of expressing the desire to know. The untenable contemporary concept that all human mental effort fundamentally arises from the instinct to preserve life and species is not in accord with the repeated observation that more is needed beyond the basic life needs. As an aside, Aristotle noted that without security and leisure, there is no expression of the desire to know.

One may go further and say that the phenomenon of life, especially human life (perhaps also forces of the inanimate cosmos as Schopenhauer claimed), is not accounted for by the hypothesis that all existence is material in nature. There appears to be something more to reality, something beyond the materialist way of thinking. This is not a question limited to theoretical physics; it extends to the very core of the human condition. Every self-aware human being intuits a force within himself that impels his activities, consciously or otherwise. This is a primary datum, antecedent to all his other information about the outer world. No worldview that does not incorporate this primary datum can be satisfying for very long. The consciousness of self as an energy is the most vivid of all consciousness, nothing else compares with it in significance.

It used to be a commonplace to observe that the scientific worldview achieves its successes by controlling nature but cannot explain the vital impulses of living creatures (*élan vital),* which in human beings is mainly manifest by a will to know. The all-but-forgotten Henri Bergson made this observation a centerpiece of his philosophy (*L'évolution créatrice*). But he, along with other thinkers who deviated from materialist dogmas by espousing metaphysical ideas, has virtually disappeared from contemporary culture. One might think that his observation would have profound significance for daily life. However, this is not the case because, in fact, *very few believe today in a metaphysical self.* The preservation and enhancement of physical life and the acquisition of material goods are the accepted routes to fulfillment because they conform to the materialist worldview. Contemporary society has been seduced by the glitter of the products of scientific technology.

A human being is what he thinks. His values are shaped by his thoughts. His ideas have consequences. If he accepts the superficial evidence of his senses and thinks there is nothing other than what they tell him then he will have materialist values no matter how he dresses them up with high-sounding phrases. If material things fascinate him, he will devote his life to them or to monetary wealth, which is the abstract representation of material things. If he does not believe the evidence of his mind that he possesses an interior self independently of interactions with the world and society, he will never devote energies to development of this self. He will remain dependent on societal definitions of success, just as a child is dependent on parental approval for his feeling of wellbeing. The disproportion between material success and personal development is the scandalous feature of "advanced" societies at the close of the twentieth century.

~ ~ ~

The idea that the materialist worldview is not adequate to the human condition is not new. The psalmist's scriptural observation that the fool in his heart says there is no God presages the development of many impassioned sermons recorded in Judeo-Christian tradition. Nevertheless, the utilitarian culture evolved in the western world during the past few centuries has served to produce outer directed individuals who are oriented toward usage of tools but not cultivation of interior being. Poverty of material circumstances is combated but there is no consciousness of poverty of the interior self. Creating an estate seems to be more important than creating a self. If there is no belief in a self, no value given to it, how can energies be directed toward its development?

The mind-body problem is the great intellectual issue for scientists of our times. Attention needs to be paid to terminology since the English language is very vague when it comes to characterizing the interior self. It is necessary to remember that words like *spirit, soul, intellect, psyche, personality, will, mind, self, consciousness, emotions, feelings, conscience* all refer to the same essential concept of an interior state distinct from physical being. The German language contains the word *Geist* that better encompasses these meanings than any equivalent in English. Perhaps this is why German philosophers have usually delved deeper into the nature of the human condition than their English-speaking analogues.

Brain scientists, who shrink from recognizing the primary reality of the self, regard it as an epiphenomenon secondary to organized cellular activity of the brain. This in itself is a metaphysical idea since the scientific mind cannot establish how or why the electrical activity of millions of individual neurons could give rise to a unitary self, epiphenomenal or otherwise. Consciousness and will of humans seem to be linked to viability of their brain but this association does not require identification of the self with the brain. It would be equally logical to attribute the growth and functions of the brain—as well as the entire body—to an antecedent energy that ultimately flowers in the appearance of a developed self. But it may be better to concede that the relationship of body and mind is beyond human ken as is the limitlessness of the universe or the infinity of time. It is enough to recognize, as did William James, that "nature in her unfathomable designs has mixed us of clay and flame, of brain and mind, that the two things hang indubitably together."

~ ~ ~

The puritanical spirit still energizes commercial life in the United States and its spirit now moves the entire civilized world. It is Puritanism minus the Christian trappings and minus the disdain of fleshly pleasures. But it is still Puritanism in that it is energized by a belief that the capitalist way is sanctioned by higher powers and that success in business is the sign of a virtuous spirit. All the innate will to individual development is channeled into the competition of the market. The world is to be conquered

91

through trade, and finally, as R. H. Tawney observed, profit making becomes a duty through which God is served (*Religion and the Rise of Capitalism*). Those same characteristics that marked the puritan mark the modern capitalist—discipline, focus, unscrupulousness, and a nerveless will to economic power. Sloth is the ultimate sin and contemplation not joined to immediate action a sign of a degenerating spirit.

Like the religious puritans, however, the puritans of the market place are headed for a fall. Religious Puritanism lost its hold as an organized form of societal life because its austerity, rigidity, and dogmatism were not in accord with the freely developing human spirit. People wanted to experience life in all its fullness; they did not want to be bound down by rigid prohibitions against all personal expression. The individual spirit wants to develop itself in every way available to it. This spirit became the American way standing for freedom of individual development in all spheres of life. But economic Puritanism, whereby personal success is measured by accumulation of wealth in all its forms, ultimately requires the denial of the interior self. There is a finite amount of energy available to the individual; if it is all expended on the exterior world, there is none left for interior development. Denial of the existence of the interior self, the "soul" of an earlier terminology, permits the individual to totally attend to the demands of economic success. These grow ever more imperious as technology increases exponentially in all aspects of civilized life. The scriptural question "what profit is to be found if a man gains the whole world and loses his own soul?" is dealt with by denying the existence of the soul.

As in every avenue of human effort, success is dependent upon meeting the demands of reality and the ability of the individual to coordinate his efforts with the reality of his being. If the metaphysical self, called the soul, is an epiphenomenon, merely an illusory appearance generated by the electrical currents of networks of neurons, then the economic model of human existence has every prospect of success since it is in accord with underlying human nature. Whether it be socialist or capitalist, or a mixture of the two, the economic model will be the blueprint of future human life. Earning and spending will define human activities in the same way that the direction of electrical currents in the brain defines the human spirit. However, if there is something more to human reality than material being, then this model will prove to be inadequate. There is growing reason to believe that this is the case.

~ ~ ~

The case of Søren Kierkegaard—The life and productivity of this individual must be one of the strangest events in the history of western literature. Kierkegaard was the quintessential misfit who defies placement either in philosophy, religion, or historical periods. He is commonly regarded as the originator of the philosophical movement known as existentialism but there is no subsequent 'existentialist' writer who even vaguely resembles him. His father was a brooding religious fanatic who imprinted his personality on his young son; most of Kierkegaard's siblings died in their youth and he himself was prey to recurrent depression. He seemed to have acquired a spinal deformity that may have had something to do with his death at 42 years of age. Most of his published works reveal an incredible verbosity in which sarcasm and irony characterize his style. His obsession with the Christian religion seems to be a direct consequence of the influence of his father. One might think that what is needed for an appreciation of Kierkegaard is a psychiatric consultation rather than literary evaluation.

However, all this is inconsequential when measured against the truly remarkable achievement of Kierkegaard in focusing on the importance of the self, the interior individual, in a European society increasingly preoccupied with cultural and scientific institutions. As well as possessing profound philosophical insights, he was a brilliant writer, capable of expounding and developing an idea as few others could. In the *Concluding Unscientific Postscript*, he defined truth as *subjectivity*, a concept that today is so politically incorrect that few can take it seriously. The primary reality for Kierkegaard was the human personality; all other considerations were merely the nuts and bolts of routine life that surrounded him in commercial Copenhagen, a traditional market town. Unfortunately, his need to connect his values with "Christianity" preoccupied him all his life and he ended it as a fanatical crusader against the state-established evangelical church of Denmark. Kierkegaard should be remembered, however, for his exposition of the significance of the human individual; all else with him is largely the smoke and wind of his eccentric personality.

~ ~ ~

A person's writing style is like his signature or his fingerprint; it defines his personality and gives insight into his depths. "The style is the man" is not a phrase coined by an esthete or a philosopher but by the noted eighteenth-century biologist Buffon. A discerning reader can quickly distinguish between the practiced style of the professional or commercial writer and the style of the writer who is oriented toward creating and unveiling his interior self. In the creation of a persona, an act that may be regarded as the birth of metaphysical individuality, writing has a role similar to speaking. The fact that it has many other roles in daily life does not negate this special feature of the human condition. Presumably Rembrandt used the same hand to paint his masterpieces as he did to feed himself or wipe his rear but no one has difficulty recognizing the importance of his dominant hand in creating his pictorial art. So it is that the written word can bring the ideas and personality of a writer into objective existence. One intuits the importance of these phenomena although there is no logical reason why it should be so. If the intuition is ignored, however, human life becomes largely mechanical in nature. As Kierkegaard has said, human beings become talking-machines instead of individuals. The distinction is readily made by anyone who is familiar with the difference between machines and people.

Genuine literary style means expression of self without regard for an assumed reader. It must be so because there is an inherent contradiction in writing for self-development as opposed to writing for readers. Of course, someone who wishes to make his living by writing cannot afford to follow this line of thought. It is necessary to feed oneself and wipe one's rear in the life into which human beings find themselves thrown. But the genuinely significant writers of the world have principally written for themselves, not for their readers. If an individual does not place the development of his own interior self ahead of the supposed needs of presumed readers, little can be expected of him in the long run as a creative writer.

~ ~ ~

Reality is the central concept which guides self-development and towards which the will directs itself. The passion for the self to align itself with reality is the lodestar of human efforts; one might also add there is a passion to create new realities. Whether it is possessed or created is irrelevant, the fact is that most individuals passionately desire to participate in the real world. The problem is in deciding where reality is to be found. Falseness and illusion appear to be everywhere. As Thoreau said with his Yankee wit, what is needed is a *realometer* that will tell the individual when he is onto the real thing. People resist the cynical idea that reality is what a person wants it to be or what the world believes it to be. There is no escape from the distinction between truth and falsity, reality and illusion, between the real world and a make-believe one.

The great delusion in most societies is that reality is only to be found in the material world and that the analytic-objectivizing approach is how this reality can be discovered. This notion has been long recognized to be erroneous because deep-thinking individuals from the beginning of recorded history discerned that the material world provides only limited access to the spectrum of reality available to *Homo sapiens*. It has become a most seductive delusion since it is based today upon the amazing accomplishments of scientific technology, a technique that has erected a material civilization beyond the wildest dreams of individuals of earlier times. A key feature of this delusion is that it is based on the ability to dominate nature. This fascinates many people who ought to know better. It is like an infatuation with youth and attractiveness in which the erotic impulse overwhelms rational thought and wisdom. At bottom, our consumer civilization is founded upon an infatuation with the products of technology that appear to be the answer to all human needs. But the assumption is untrue and cannot endure because it is not founded on metaphysical reality just as a physical infatuation will not in the long run be sufficient for a developed personality. The tragedy of our times is that the finite energies of the individual are wasted upon the seductive appeal of technology.

Although technology along with the scientific-analytic mentality that creates it has allowed many individuals to go beyond the biological requirements of survival in nature and has expanded physical horizons in a manner unknown to former eras, the limitations of this mentality are becoming evident to those who have the vision to see them. A Faustian bargain has its price; humans are more and more condemned to the hell of unmitigated technological existence. What is worse is the lack of awareness that this is indeed a hell, that a human existence lacking metaphysical being is a hell for human beings. Selling the possibility of creating one's own soul is the price for unrestrained technological development. Faust at least made his bargain as a mature personality, in full possession of his faculties. Today, this bargain is foisted upon children before they have the possibility of making an informed decision. The concept of the reality of metaphysical existence is not communicated to children today. Even more pertinently, the example is not provided by the adults who nurture them. It is this sense of metaphysical emptiness that is at the heart of the devout Christian's objection to secular schooling. It is a valid objection albeit it is doubtful that conventional religious instruction can repair it. There is little gain in replacing one delusional worldview with another.

~ ~ ~

The avoidance of commitment to an interior self by educated and affluent individuals is a very singular phenomenon. It is one thing to be so overwhelmed by the requirements of survival that there is no time or energy to attend to interior needs; it is quite another to deliberately direct one's attentions away from this aspect of the self. Consciousness of self is such an immediate intuition that it is a cause for astonishment to see it so neglected in formative years by so many able, energetic individuals. Perhaps the seductive attractions of technology noted above accounts for this neglect to some degree. However, beyond this factor, one can discern another, perhaps more potent reason for neglect of interior being. This is a *fear of the metaphysical self* that can be noticed by a perceptive onlooker.

Human beings can control surrounding nature to a remarkable extent since nature is usually no match for the human ingenuity except in its extreme manifestations. However, the metaphysical self is another matter as it is not subject to material control through predictable means. A more subtle approach is required. Even more disconcerting may be the realization that there are inborn features of the self that cannot be altered. Who can say to what extent the capacity for consciousness of reality is subject to human control? Perhaps there are individuals who are inherently capable of a metaphysical consciousness denied to another; perhaps there are even races or genders so endowed. One of the major philosophical questions of the antique era was whether virtue could be taught. Plato's theory of knowledge as recollection is well known; it goes without saying that he was referring to philosophical knowledge or consciousness. Anyone can learn to fire a gun or drive an automobile. Perhaps the dominant peoples of today are incapable of metaphysical knowledge; consequently, they deny the existence of the soul and all that emanates from it.

Or, perhaps, too much attention paid to science and technology in early life permanently impairs spiritual capacity. If this be true, it is frightening to imagine the consequences of computer training of the young, frightening to think of the possibility of stunting the distinctive metaphysical capacities of humans.

All this may appear quite "unreal" to those who fundamentally believe in the reality of the brain and disbelieve in the reality of the soul. Maintenance of a monistic worldview becomes a self-fulfilling prophecy that ultimately leads to a purely mechanical way of life devoid of metaphysical substance. It is unlikely that the leaders of technological societies will acquire the wisdom exhibited by the leaders of Erewhon in the remarkably prescient novel of that name by Samuel Butler. There the fictitious rulers recognized the pernicious effects of unlimited technology and banned all new machines from their society. However, Butler lived in the nineteenth century when it was still possible to fully encompass the effects of technology on society.

It is depressing to consider the world we live in when reflecting on individual needs. Kierkegaard repeats over and over that the "crowd" is always in the wrong. Our civilization is the crowd, it is always in the wrong, it is always acting against the welfare of the individual. There is no use in pointing to the benefits provided by society; these are another matter existing on a level having to do with biological and social needs. When a deadly infection destroys an individual in his prime, there is little consolation in thinking the same natural forces that destroyed the individual provide the oxygen and nourishment necessary for life. The infection needs to be combated with all the power and resourcefulness available to the individual. So it is that the deadly effects of social pressures on the soul need to be combated by every available force and resource.

~ ~ ~

Religious and other metaphysical forms of consciousness have always been a principal feature of a civilized human state. Even the ancient Greek Cynics believed in the sanctity of the mind. The question arises as to what is religious consciousness? For the one committed to monistic materialism, it is a form of superstition or illusion, having to do with the well-known capacity of people for self-deception. It is viewed as the successor to the primitive animism of stone-age man. The title of Freud's essay, *Future of an Illusion*, represents the underlying attitude toward religious dogmas by most scientifically educated individuals. At best, they are thought of as illustrating the capacity for imaginative thinking and belong in the same category as other imaginative products of the fertile human mind. This point of view is founded on the bedrock belief of our times that physical being is the sum total of existence. What cannot be analyzed physically does not exist. It goes without saying that the notion of a physical deity is an absurdity to the modern mind.

Yet religious consciousness is persistent and pervasive. The conviction of the scientific humanists of the nineteenth century that organized religions were destined to soon disappear has not turned out to be correct. A resurgent Islam is making its presence felt everywhere and Christianity is exerting more influence than ever in contemporary affairs. Hinduism gains strength constantly amidst one billion subcontinent Indians. The advances of technology have not impeded the progress of organized religions. There is a simple and obvious explanation for the persistent manifestations of religion within 'developed' as well as undeveloped societies. It is that individuals have the will to develop themselves as metaphysical beings and not merely pieces of biological or sociological machinery. They are not satisfied to be talking-machines whose only need is to have their mechanisms well lubricated and their parts replaced as necessary. Nor are they satisfied to have cultural history define their being. There is a metaphysical need in a human that requires satisfaction; among his many features there stands out the principal one, he is a metaphysical animal. There is no reason to regard this feature as any more illusory than his biological or social needs; there is no reason to categorize the one as reality but the other as illusion. At the root of it all, existence for a living creature is his efforts to fulfill his desires which he may label as instinct or illusion but the one has no more basis in logic than the other. Human beings have a natural piety, a natural yearning toward eternity, a natural reverence for a spiritual reality whose manifestations they intuit. No materialist view of the world accounts for the will to develop a metaphysical existence.

Religious consciousness is one thing; religious creeds are another. How is one to define the metaphysical need that is encountered in the depths of the self? Modern religions are based on the notion of an all-powerful cosmic being who is called God or some cognate in the Judeo-Christian-Islamic tradition. Christianity maintains that a religious consciousness leads to the knowledge of God, but this is possible only through faith in his "son" Jesus Christ. Other religions have their own routes to the knowledge of deity. The common denominator is the conviction that the metaphysical need is fulfilled by consciousness of one's relationship with God. God conceived as the all-pervasive, all-powerful force underlying existence. Dogmatic religions feel that they have the key to a God-relationship. But it is very dubious that any institutions created and maintained by humans could have possession of such a key.

The philosopher Friedrich Nietzsche was possessed by a consuming religious consciousness that he could not relate to religious creeds. Hatred of Christianity became an obsession with him that must have contributed to his mental breakdown. In *Thus Spoke Zarathustra*, which may be viewed as his personal confession of faith, Nietzsche proclaimed that he was in love with "eternity" (*Ewigkeit*). Later he had many other things to say on the subject, but the form of his own religious consciousness is best seen in his most famous work. Eternity for him was not a temporal phenomenon but a property of his consciousness. Truly creative thinkers like Bergson, Berdyaev, and Heidegger recognized that placing the concept of time in proper perspective is an essential aspect of metaphysical consciousness. In the case of Kierkegaard, one has the feeling that his God is an imaginary companion who has replaced his strange relationship with his natural father. It seems to be a mental prop he needed to carry out the project of thought that has become a milestone of western metaphysical consciousness.

~ ~ ~

The concept of a universal God is encumbered with too many untenable historical associations to satisfy a developed consciousness. There is in *Homo sapiens* an intellectual consciousness as well as a religious one. This is the basis of the humanistic denial of religion. The word "God" can no longer serve as the expression of a metaphysical need without one falling into insoluble conflicts with contemporary creeds. There are very few today who claim God speaks to them; honest individuals who have strained every fiber to hear his voice have described the silence experienced by them. Hardly anyone continues to listen; rather, belief in God's existence is accepted by rote as part of a traditional faith while going about the daily tasks of material living. It may well be that the traditional beliefs stand in the way of a true religious consciousness; they may impede the personal metaphysical development that is the only real route to satisfaction of the metaphysical need—if one can speak of satisfaction in this area. Kierkegaard, for example, conceived of suffering as the only really characteristic sign of a religious consciousness.

Reverence for the metaphysical self is a better focus for fulfillment of the metaphysical need than is reverence for life, God, or any of the latter's self-proclaimed representatives. Nietzsche wrote that reverence of self is the mark of the noble personality but it is more likely that one becomes noble through this reverence. One can debate the sequence of events. However, if there is any validity to the idea that self-development is possible, then reverence for the interior self is the most pressing need of the individual in an age dominated by technology values.

The word "mysticism" is often used in a disparaging manner. Today, mystical thinking is a pejorative term referring to one who has not been sufficiently disciplined to the requirements of objective, analytical thought. There is a seeming refusal to acknowledge that consciousness itself is a mystical state since the idea of consciousness has no material basis. One proceeds with difficulty from neuronal circuitry to consciousness. This is why it is so often viewed as illusory by those who think about these things in a scientific manner. However, the more important question is what one does with this mystical consciousness and how it serves the creation of self.

Suspended consciousness without some directive purpose as supposedly recommended in the Buddhist way of life must be regarded with great suspicion. There is something inhuman about the concept. There is always a goal in human behavior whether it be conquest of the world or emancipation from its demands. Neither goal by itself necessarily leads to self-development but may be part of a program leading to it. The danger with either is losing sight of the ultimate purpose of metaphysical development.

The will to develop the self through experience, learning, and expression is just as much a mystical phenomenon as is any form of introverted withdrawal. There is no objective reason or scientific justification for elaboration of consciousness other than the manifestly inadequate claim that all mental activity somehow serves the need for biological survival. But even the doctrine of an instinct for preservation of self and species is a mystical idea not explicable by any known law of physics. There is no "scientific" reason why living organisms should strive to maintain themselves through millions of years, endlessly refining and replicating genetic codes in spite of the hazards involved. The laws of physics would lead one to expect the opposite; an accumulation of 'entropy' or constant tendency toward the breaking down of complex structures. A mystical force for life is required, which is the will to survive and develop, the *élan vital* of Bergson. Recognition of the will to develop a soul is merely a step further in this mystical thinking; it is a step further in consciousness of the human condition.

Experience, learning, understanding, speaking out, writing down—all these processes act to enhance the interior self. Disconnection from the external world limits the development of the interior self. Sartre was right in claiming that some form of *engagement* is required to give meaning to life; this meaning is self-development. Selection of the form of *engagement* is the difficult problem of the human condition requiring a knowledge of self that can never be fully adequate. One thing is certain as Thoreau somewhere noted; forms of *engagement* founded on the making of money invariably lead the self on a downward path.

~ ~ ~

Spirituality can be defined as valuing an interior metaphysical self. To be spiritual is to act in such a manner as to develop that self as opposed to gaining material ends. Broadening of the mind, experiential development, creative expression—all these things that individuals do to enlarge themselves—represent the process of becoming spiritual. Humility, self-abnegation, and charity are possible stages on the road to reevaluation of what is important; they are not ends in their own right.

In an era of fabulous technology, worship of origins and traditions becomes a metaphysical refuge, an escape from the responsibility of creating an interior self. Admittedly, one's appearance, habits, attitudes, behaviors, and language may be all more or less carry-overs from past generations but these are simply the external accoutrements of the soul. If there is such a thing as an interior self then there is by definition a material shell encasing it. The purpose of human life, however, is missed when all the focus is on the shell. What advantage can there be in emphasizing external styles or roles which one has had no part in creating? For human beings with a soul, role-playing is acting not living.

The preoccupation with roots, ethnicity, and ancestral customs that is so prevalent subsequent to the repudiation of nationalism and communism is an admission of bankruptcy of self. It is the logical consequence of having been persuaded that the self is an ignorant or sinful delusion. When the materialist view of the human condition is accepted, there is nothing left to revere but the bones of dead ancestors. Biological inheritance is all that remains if the soul does not exist. In America, in spite of overwhelming technological superiority, it is difficult to find genuine self-respect in individuals, regardless of their being wealthy, poor, or middle-class. There is a constant concern with validating one's life through offspring or monumental do-goodisms. But what can be the justification of foisting one's duties onto children or trying to do good elsewhere when the chief responsibility of one's life, the creation of a soul, has been neglected?

The contemporary western world refers to the search for spirituality outside of traditional faiths as New Age religion. But "New Age" movements date back to the dawn of recorded history. Isaiah and Jesus were New Age prophets. Buddhism, Christianity, and Islam started out as New Age religions. New Age phenomena have been found in all eras, sometimes they are referred to as mysticism. Sufiism, Kaballah, Swedenborgianism, Theosophy, Christian Science, Shamanism, Voodooism are some ancient and modern varieties of New Age thought. There is no historical period in which certain individuals did not react against the materialism of the day by founding new forms of spirituality. Fraud and commercialism have always infected New Age movements. Most have had something significant to contribute to the human condition. Yet, however, at the end of the day, the individual cannot look to organized movements to create his own soul. This is a task that only he can accomplish; there are no formulae that will provide him with ready-made solutions. It is valuing the spiritual self and the will to assume full responsibility for its development that will count in an unseen but ever-present scheme of being.

~ ~ ~

Very few societies support the metaphysical aspirations of an individual. Generally they require it to be in tune with the cultural or religious ideals prevalent at the time. The ancient Greeks were unusual in that they gradually came to espouse the philosophic life as the supreme virtue. The image of Socrates cultivated after his death embodied this ideal. Its force was so great that it dominated Roman culture even while Greece was politically subject to Rome. The rise of Christianity and its establishment as a state religion ended Greek philosophy as a cultural force in the Roman world with the Christian idea of God enthroned as the dominant ideal. One can debate the reasons for this change but the fact is well established. The western world still lives under the influence of this event although its influence has diminished.

With the European renaissance came a technological civilization that replaced Christianity as the dominant ideal of the western world. Instead of thought or piety, technology is the mark of civilized progress. While the rest of the world may have rejected European imperialism, it has fallen under the sway of European culture, most strikingly demonstrated in America. It seems almost a reflex response that exposure to Euro-American technology brings forth an imitative response in all the peoples of the planet. It may be a special trait of the human condition that it strives to make its life more and more technological in nature. It is this phenomenon that produces the worldwide psychology of consumerism enriching global corporations.

However, it is difficult to believe that human beings will remain permanently infatuated with the products of technology. Aside from all the ecological arguments, the infatuation requires faith that technological products are intrinsically valuable and identifiable with the needs of individual development. The moment this faith wavers, the world market will crumble into the dust from which it arose. The religious ideal has proven to be impotent to counter this faith. Devotion to technology arose because commitment to Christian dogmas did not meet the requirement of reality; it is unrealistic, therefore, to think at this late date the process can be reversed. A new ideal and a new will is necessary which will be more closely founded on the requirements of human reality. One is entitled to imagine that this new ideal will be the development of a metaphysical self.

~ ~ ~

The key intellectual problem of modern times is how one conceives of a metaphysical will to self-development in light of the objective findings of scientific geology, astronomy, physics, and biology. How does one reconcile the felt powers of the interior self with the vastness of object existence uncovered by scientific instruments? It is a question largely ignored in an object-oriented culture. The time is long past when a von Kleist reading Kant could become depressed to the point of suicide over the smallness of the human condition. If the reality of self is confined to its physical dimensions, there really seems little point in worrying about its development.

One might compare the issue to the problem of the dramatic art in the cinema. An enormous technology is required to bring forth a film in today's cultural climate. There is the initial investment, the technology of production, the expertise of the supporting staff, the necessities of marketing, the advertising techniques all of which are required to bring success at the box office. Sometimes this success seems to occur through the sheer power of technology in conveying sensory images. But without the force of an indwelling *idea* to which all the material elements contribute, any temporary appeal soon loses its interest to viewers. There is no reality to it. For *Homo sapiens,* there is no reality to anything that does not relate to the human spirit. Human reality is metaphysically based; activities not founded on this truth will not long endure.

One cannot look to the past for models that serve the present. Knowledge of the past is of value only insofar as it enlivens one to move to a new future. Life is a dangerous game surrounded by constant threats of extinction. This is as true of the interior self as it is of the physical body. The soul is not a static being; it continually changes for the better or the worse. Growth or decay characterizes all living beings. It is not limited to the biological, i.e., material substrate, since there is a metaphysical substrate that lies behind the biological one. The seventeenth century religious mystic Jacob Boehme viewed all material being as the 'signature' of an underlying metaphysical reality, this is essentially also the view of more recent profound thinkers like Nicolai Berdyaev and Teilhard de Chardin. If it is uniquely given to humans to have a consciousness of this reality, it is incumbent upon them to develop the capacity for it. Animals can enjoy life but only humans can wonder if they are enjoying it. This "wonder" is not a biological epiphenomenon; it is a metaphysical reality.

~ ~ ~

In his usual ironical manner, Søren Kierkegaard proposed a definition of abstract thought as thought without a thinker. What he meant to emphasize is that there is no thought without an underlying passion, i.e., a will that powers the thought process. *Homo faber* prefers not to waste energy analyzing his passions; rather, he commonly conceals them behind a façade of well-meaning utilitarianism. The most objective, unbiased, analytical scientific mind is powered in its activity by a passion habitually concealed. It is no secret that the commonplace desires for fame, prestige, and monetary gain motivate the great technological innovators much as they did the explorers and conquistadors of former times. Today the more subtle pleasures of societal acclaim are being replaced by the raw desire for wealth. Patents, not personal monuments, are becoming the chief goal of scientific researchers and technological innovators.

The moral motivations are little different than the more obvious material ones. After the most penetrating analysis of Christianity, the philosopher Nietzsche concluded that the underlying motivation of the movement was a will to power. He did not exclude its apotheosized founder. The most fervent benefactor of the poor and dispossessed is personally empowered in some way by his activities, whether it be by accumulating credits in heaven or establishing himself more forcefully in the world below. According to contemporary socio-biologists, all acts of altruism are motivated by the desire to establish the security of one's own kith and kin. Altruism is put in the category of a biological instinct.

Nothing is to be gained, however, by disparaging the personal motivations of the most scientific or altruistic of individuals. The self is at the root of all willed behavior; what is significant is the quality of the motivations that drive its affairs. It is how one conceives personal development, consciously or unconsciously, which is the mark of the person and which establishes his "nobility" or lack thereof. There are no objective or revelatory criteria to determine this quality; there is only the perspective of the individual who is embarked upon his own life. The instinct to personal development is wholly dependent for its realization upon the perspectives of the individual. If man is not the measure of all things, he is certainly the only measure available for human scrutiny. Thus the real question in the life of *Homo sapiens* is how he proposes to develop himself. It should not have to be said that limiting oneself to a purely materialist perspective is a recipe for personal disaster.

~ ~ ~

It is simpler to develop the self in terms of objective or external realities than in terms of its metaphysical nature. One can count his money, envision his property, and even quantitatively assess his reputation. In the world of academia, there is a device for counting how many times a

111

researcher is cited in the professional literature. It is widely used for decisions on promotion and tenure. Counting publications is a longstanding means for evaluation of university faculty. In the entertainment world, there are quantitative means for rating popularity; sports figures have the endless statistics to measure their performance. Without measurement, nothing is accepted, including performance of executives, teachers, and ministers. The main subject for debate is what needs to be measured in order to evaluate the performer. These measures are utilized not merely by controlling authorities but by the individual himself who has been habituated to quantitate his success in life.

But personal metaphysical development is not subject to quantitative analysis. Intuition cannot be quantified in order to evaluate 'success' in life. There are no objective criteria; in fact, objective signs of success are often a clue to the impoverishment of the individual. This is evident in the activities of many societally successful individuals who, having expended their energies in societal competition, become aware that something is missing in their existence. They begin to realize that they may have missed the fundamental goal of human individual development. It is often too late because there is nothing that interferes more with the personality than monetary wealth or celebrity status. There is truth to the gospel adage about the relative difficulties of camels and the well-to-do in performing certain transitions (Mt. 19:23-24).

Finally, there are the diversions offered by the worship of something outside the interior self. Sometimes this is called discovering one's cultural identity. It may be worship of one's ancestors, traditional faith, nature, science, esthetics, and, most especially, a concept of deity. Any one or combination of these can serve to divert oneself from the difficult problem of interior development. Nicolai

Berdyaev in his remarkable work *Slavery and Freedom* has elaborated on these diversions which he calls forms of slavery. Whatever one thinks of Berdyaev's own religious attitudes, he possessed a consciousness of metaphysical reality that deserves a more important place in literary culture than it has heretofore received. Berdyaev was a great pioneer in explorations of the interior self.

It is important to recognize the fact that excessive attention to self is regarded as a fault in Judeo-Christian-Islamic cultures. The worship of God or his agents on earth carries with it the obvious corollary that too much attention to self is a moral error if not a sin. The terms selfish, self-centered, self-seeking, self-satisfied all carry pejorative connotations. They indicate an individual with a faulty compass in life; his attention is thought to be focused in the wrong direction, toward the self instead of toward God, Christ, humanity, the public good, the poor and needy, etc., etc. It is not acknowledged that attention to self, *amour de soi* in the words of Rousseau, is "the sole passion natural to man." It is a fundamental instinct in living beings, which in man takes a more highly developed form than in any other living creature. It can no more be suppressed than can the drives to breathe, drink, eat or sexually couple without incurring adverse consequences. The real issue is how attention to self is expressed, not that it is there at all because its absence is a sign of a moribund individual. Narcissistic preoccupation with the physical self, the societal self, the self as a celebrity figure is corruption of the indwelling instinct for development of an interior self which gives a person a distinctively human face.

This need to develop the interior self has been radically altered in technological societies that turn all their energies to inanimate machines and consciously or unconsciously attempt to make humans resemble them.

What writer could say today as Herman Melville did in *Moby-Dick:* "Men may seem detestable as joint-stock companies and nations; knaves, fools, and murderers there may be; men may have mean and meagre faces; but man, in the ideal, is so noble and sparkling, such a grand and glowing creature, that over any ignominious blemish in him all his fellows should run to throw their costliest robes." Melville did not come to a happy end in nineteenth century America that valued joint-stock companies more than the ideal of man but at least it was possible for him to express his vision. Today such a thought appears impossibly romantic, childish at best. The concept would not be taken seriously.

~ ~ ~

But at the end of the day, reality is victorious over all other competitors in the realm of human affairs. The real world is an object of desire that brooks no rivals. The naïve idea, however, that the real world is only that which one can touch, feel, or otherwise sensuously experience is an idea that needs to be relegated to the domain of childhood where it belongs. It is a passing stage in the development of a human being. If there are some who do not wish to emerge from childhood, so be it, but they do not deserve adulation. Somewhere Kierkegaard says that a spiritual relationship of one flesh and blood individual with another is impossible of attainment. This may seem a perverse statement by one who aspired to be a Christian but it expresses the basic truth that Kierkegaard perceived, namely that interior development was the only route to spirituality. He and other Christian mystics conceive of this development in terms of a relationship with God; but the latter concept can be readily replaced by another—such as *Worldspirit,*

Brahman, the *Over-Soul*—or any others that one might prefer. It would be foolish to deny the possibility of a transcendent force underlying the human condition. However, the task of an individual is to elaborate his own soul, not its relationship to what is impossible for the human mind to encompass.

This awareness was the driving force of the existential movement in philosophy. The work of Martin Heidegger even with his laborious German scholasticism is an expression of this awareness. Heidegger forgot the dictum of Kierkegaard that all abstract thought requires the presence of a passionate thinker. For this reason, regardless of translation, Heidegger seems to be writing in a foreign language for those who are unused to the obscurities of German philosophical language. The passion that powered Heidegger is hard to find but those who discern it regard him as one of the profoundest representatives of twentieth century thought.

Passion behind the thought is what distinguishes human beings from talking machines. There are those who believe passion is a dangerous quality in the realm of human thought, that it can lead to the gas chambers of Auschwitz as well as to idealistic writings. Its dangers cannot be ignored. There is nothing more worthy of ridicule, however, than the well-known photograph of Adolf Hitler contemplating a bust of Nietzsche. Passion for Nietzsche, as for all genuinely spiritual thinkers, was in the service of the interior self, not the race, nation, disadvantaged classes, or any other external category that can seduce the interest of unwary individuals. Eternity is what Nietzsche loved; it was certainly not the Aryan race. The glorification of technology can be seen in this regard as just another effort to evade the inner self by concentrating attention on the world of *materia* in which technique and property replace interior experience. The materialist *Weltanschauung* may have internal coherence but it is not in accord with the realities of human existence. Reality ultimately is disclosed only to the metaphysical inner self through the development of personality and understanding rather than quantitative adaptations to the world of *materia* with all its devices. There is no escape from the interior self without the proliferation of self-defeating pathological features in the individual.

~ ~ ~

Metaphysical development is impossible without leisure. Aristotle commented that leisure is an essential prerequisite for the highest form of happiness, which he thought was pursuit of knowledge for its own sake. Since Aristotle was not politically correct by modern standards, he did not hesitate to state this was only possible for an elite few; the masses of mankind were slavish by nature requiring crude entertainment for their happiness. The higher type of men, however, who shared divine qualities with the Gods, wished to enlarge their scope through knowledge. The embodiment of this type of man was the Greek philosopher.

It is matter for irony that the leisure that was thought to be a prerequisite for a higher life during antiquity is becoming just what is most deficient in contemporary technology-based living. If there is one thing social critics agree upon today, it is that during the prime of their life, most people are too busy. There are some who feel gratified by hectic societal activity; most individuals, however, sense themselves to be overly pressed by the requirements of life at the turn of the twentieth century. Only the poor and the elderly have leisure; but, as previously noted, by then their habits of life rarely include development of the interior self. Time on the golf course, not self-development, is the customary goal of American retirement. Slavish habits of a lifetime cannot be altered by a signature on a retirement application.

Technology may prolong life, facilitate travel, expand information acquisition, or furnish entertainment but leisure it does not provide. The invention of the internal combustion engine, television, computers, and all the other magic-like products of human ingenuity have increased the demands on the individual rather than his leisure hours. One might imagine that this state of affairs would engender a revolution of the oppressed people. But the opposite seems true—technology is embraced with open arms, worshipped, and loved, just as the Russian ruling class of old were venerated by the serfs as long as they were treated with a modicum of decency. Technology is identified with affluent living and is democratically open to all so it has become an object of veneration by virtually the entire world.

Nevertheless, leisure is what is needed by *Homo sapiens,* however narrowly or broadly one wishes to interpret this term. Man in the ideal as defined by Melville cannot sparkle and glow without the availability of large swaths of leisure time and the capacity to utilize it for the purpose inherent in him. Slavish living, whether the master is a man or a machine, whether it be imposed by force or be self-imposed, is a cause for shame and a reason for radical alteration of any society in which it is prevalent. A long life marked by slavery to *materia* is hardly to be preferred to a short one; availability of shelter, sustenance, and security does not alter this judgment, the same was usually true of black slavery in the South. A putative freedom that does not provide leisure is no freedom at all. It is a sham to cover the shameful condition of slavery.

A principal reason technological slavery flourishes is that human beings have been persuaded that their souls do not exist. If there is no interior self, no metaphysical form of being, there is no reason to bemoan the absence of leisure. Machines function best when they are working, when they are not, they rust and deteriorate. All that is needed are lubricants and occasional repair of worn out parts. All machines are replaceable. This is exactly how humans are treated in technological society except that when they no longer function optimally they enter museum-like retirement centers instead of immediately converted to scrap. There is no help for this state of affairs as long as individuals are not devoted to an interior self that takes priority over all other things. A society valuing technology above the soul did not arise of its own accord, it is the result of conscious decisions made by its members. If it is true that the profit motive is at the heart of all technological development, it is also true that most consumers unconsciously *worship* many products of technology. As long as this devotion is maintained, technological living will flourish.

~ ~ ~

One consequence of leisure is the deepening of the desire to worship. Genuine worship expresses the will to align the self with a transcendental reality—intuited or imagined according to one's point of view. It represents the ultimate in an "existential report" to use a phrase coined by Kierkegaard. It is a thought process diametrically opposed to what occurs in objective analysis, which is why science and religion can never have anything but the most superficial of relationships. However much one can be indoctrinated in worship procedures, the sense of a transcendental reality arises from the interior self and is not the outcome of a training process.

If the inborn desire for worship does not find a metaphysical symbol, it invariably will find a material one, e.g., money, machines, race, status, celebrity figures, and so on to the most insignificant of material phenomena. Thus, adult individuals can be found who make symbols of worship out of sports figures, entertainers, or politicians. If reverence for self is not somehow translated into a reverence for the transcendental, it too becomes corrupted into narcissistic trivialities. It is quite amazing to see what intelligent human beings are capable of treating as objects of worship. Idolatry is the term that historically has been used to designate worship of *materia*. It is to the credit of the Judeo-Christian-Islamic religions that they do not sanction idolatry, even if the symbolism of Christian institutions sometimes seems indistinguishable from mere idolatry.

The process of worship can be described as long as one does not confuse the analysis with the phenomenon. Description of a sex act is not the same as engaging in it. Worship needs to be confined to the intuition of a transcendental reality. It is a metaphysical experience that is the natural consequence of an awareness of a metaphysical self; thus, if one is not aware of his own metaphysical self, there is little chance that he can become aware of a transcendental reality, which is necessarily metaphysical in nature. By *aware* is meant an experience beyond the mere wordplay contained in traditional faiths. The highest use of the mind is the effort to express the intuition of a metaphysical reality. Such use of the mind requires the development of self and is not simply automatic in human beings.

There is an ancient anecdote that the Greek philosopher Thales fell into a cistern while he was reflecting on the meaning of the starry sky above him. The fall was witnessed by a Thracian maid who helped him climb out of the cistern. The tale may have been meant to indicate that her sense of reality was greater than was his. But as long as reality is conceived as avoiding accidents and controlling nature, there is no hope for *Homo sapiens.* Like rats in small cages, sooner or later they fall to attacking each other. The world of metaphysical reality is a *terra incognita* more needful of exploration than Mars or Venus. Existential thought is the most recent term given to this exploration whose antecedents go back to the origins of western philosophy and the forest sages of India. The name of Kierkegaard will always have a prominent place in the history of this thought. More than any other recent literary figure, he focused on the centrality of an interior self in a proper conception of human beings. We can forgive his prolixity, his intellectual contortions in trying to identify Christianity with a transcendental reality, his dubious resort to "pseudo-anonymous" authorship. He got the main thing right, which is that the development of an interior self is more important than all the societal accomplishments of famous people or well-meaning functionaries. A little essay published by him toward the end of his short life contains the core of the matter:

> So it is that I understand everything now. From the beginning I could not thus survey what has been in fact my own development...Before God, religiously, when I talk with myself, I call the whole literary activity my own upbringing and

development—not, however, implying that I am now perfect or completely finished so as to need no more upbringing and development.

My Activity as a Writer, 1851

This passage is a suitable epitaph to the literary effort of Søren Kierkegaard whose work deserves more widespread reflection and less scholarly analysis. It is an epitaph for any writer whose motivation stems from the hidden wellspring of human spiritual activity.

~ ~ ~

It is unfortunate that the concept of a judgment day has been relegated to the realm of superstition. Perhaps this is the fault of numerous Christian sermonizers who took too many poetical liberties with the idea, expressing in fantastic imagery that undermined its believability. A metaphysical judgment day is not to be conceived of in physical terms, however vividly they may be expressed. But that there is a significance to one's interior life which is independent of its impact on society is an intuition which no right-minded person can avoid once his mind is allowed freedom, even if the details of the process are obscure. The notion of absurd people in an absurd world is the product of the materialistic dogma dominating the mind. Judgment will be passed on what one has not made of his own self, not what sins of omission or commission he may have imposed on the world around him. Socrates feared to do wrong because of the damage it would do to his soul. In sum, we will have to account for what we have made of our inner selves. All the humanitarian activity and societal tinkering will count for little next to this one task. "Become what you can be"—

that is the single command, the one thing needful in the course of a life requiring development of a self. There may be a place for tinkering with one's environment just as there is for trash carriers, plumbers, doctors, or politicians but it is a grave error to place these activities ahead of the one thing needful. In a reality founded upon metaphysical existence, few will inquire as to how the minutiae of daily life have been handled; it will be assumed that reasonable arrangements have been made. If they were not, if plagues, wars, or premature bodily breakdown ends the life of an individual, it will only be an event that must happen sooner or later to all biological organisms. Prolonging the life of *Homo sapiens* is worthwhile to the degree that it deepens consciousness; otherwise, the effort makes no sense. Prolongation of human life without metaphysical deepening is the real absurdity of human societies.

~ ~ ~

A clear sign of the predicament of our culture is the placing of neurology ahead of metaphysics, i.e., imagining that human spirituality will be ultimately explained by neurophysiological studies. It is true that all kinds of mental states can be simulated by electrical or chemical stimulation of the brain. These include the most varied mystical states heretofore assigned to divine origins. Epileptic discharges have been described as evoking the sensation of nearness to God. These observations support the view of those who wish for whatever reason to deny the reality of a metaphysical self. The naïve materialism, whose antecedents lie in the theories of the Greek atomicists, has received a new lease on life through the experimentation of modern neurosciences.

The facts must be confronted squarely. There can be no doubt that consciousness as it is ordinarily understood is associated with neuronal processes in the brain. The observations that emotional states or mystical feelings can be triggered by chemical or electrical alterations of the brain do not mean, however, that emotions or mystical feelings are explicable through physiological investigations of the brain cell activity. The problem is a conceptual one, requiring a reordering of the usual empirical-analytic style of thought. Once one accepts that there is a multidimensional aspect to life in general and to the human condition in particular, it is not difficult to imagine the brain as the material dimension of the mind, while remembering that its mental contents express a vastly different dimension, reaching beyond the familiar physical parameters utilized by the sciences. Scientists may recoil from this concept but without it they can never hope to apprehend the meaning of the human mind. In fact, once one opens his own mind to the possibility that reality extends beyond the material world, there is no difficulty in envisioning brain and mind as two different facets of the underlying reality of self, which is the *ding-an-sich* of a thinking human being. One facet is the physiological nuts and bolts of mental activity, the other the higher meaning encompassed by it.

It is well established that the brain is an essential link in all forms of human expression. But just as the meaning of the written word cannot be found in analyzing the cellular mechanisms of muscular contractions of the hand, neither can they be found in analyzing the mechanisms of brain cellular activity, no matter how complex they may be. The fact that the brain is an essential link in mental expression does not mean that it is the generating cause of this expression. The difficulty with conceiving how the mind influences the body pales before the impossibility in conceiving how physical changes in neurons are associated with mental states. These kinds of conceptual difficulties, however, are no excuse for rejecting the intuition of self. Circumventing the content of thought may give insight into its mechanics but not into its essential meaning. In Kierkegaard's terms, there is no "existential report."

The boldness of the brain scientists and neurophilosophers in denying metaphysical reality is astonishing. Since many have lost interest or capacity for metaphysical consciousness, they wish to deny its existence. A lifetime of scientific objectivity will, no doubt, blunt the inwardness necessary to apprehend the soul. Darwin confessed he had lost the ability to appreciate poetical expression. Freud similarly recognized he had no "oceanic feelings." Contemporary scientists rarely feel the need to comment on these deficiencies. Goethe's comment placed in the mouth of Mephistopheles two centuries ago is still apropos:

> I recognize the learned scholar's speech!
> What is not there to touch is out of reach,
> What is impalpable is wholly missed,
> The incomputable does not exist,
> What you can't weigh is air upon your scale,
> What you don't coin you think does not avail.
> *Faust*, Part II (Arndt trans.)

It may be that too much time spent with the minutiae of analytic observations on the nervous system of human beings is unhealthy for one's own mind. *Docta ignorantia,* the learned ignorance approved of by the medieval philosopher Nicolaus Cusanus, is appropriate today, except that it is now applicable to brain scientists instead of scholastics.

~ ~ ~

Human beings are devious creatures. As Nietzsche pointed out, scientists and scholars are affected with the same will to power as are politicians and generals. One must be cautious in accepting 'objective' judgments of the leaders of the technological era. Emerson is a more reliable guide to the workings of the human mind then are neurophysiologists because the substance of self is not ascertainable by laboratory experimentation. It is wholly missed when approached via the tools of brain researchers. The dogma that reality can be only discovered through the study of *materia* leads to dead ends when it concerns the human self no matter how many magic-like demonstrations are conjured up to bemuse credulous audiences. Idolatry is at the core of modern technology; as Joseph Wood Krutch wrote in his *Human Nature and the Human Condition*, we seem to be hypnotized by machines, therefore, we cannot control them. He went on to say, "And we do not want to control it [the machine] because in our hearts we believe it more interesting, more wonderful, more admirable and more rich in potentialities than we ourselves are." He understated the situation; in fact, we are told that "we" do not even exist apart from the machine-like brain lodged in our cranium.

This tendency toward idolatry of *materia* is the weak link in the human condition. Out of this tendency have arisen the gigantic edifices that seem to dwarf the individual. The pyramid culture of ancient Egypt, the cathedrals of medieval Christianity, the power-laden machinery of the technological era, the magic-like contemporary computer revolution—all these developments result in losing sight of the essential fact that the will of the individual human has created them all.

Underlying it all is the self that is the antecedent and more significant reality. When a society loses sight of the priority of the self, not to speak of its very existence, then disaster is the expected consequence.

The hubris of the ancient Israelites in thinking they created a real God from molten jewelry is hardly different from the scientists of today who persuade their followers that their laboratories will solve the mysteries of the human condition. The book of E. O. Wilson entitled *Consilience* (1998) is perhaps the most comprehensive advocacy of the materialist viewpoint to appear in English in the twentieth century. Wilson has a breadth to his arguments that are rarely found in contemporary scientific popularization. A lifetime as a Harvard professor has trained him to be a balanced, reasonable, urbane writer. He summarizes the materialist view of the mind and consciousness in an unequivocal manner. It is worth quoting him:

> Consciousness is the parallel processing of vast numbers of coding networks. The synchronized firing of neurons and the simultaneous mapping of multiple sensory impressions create "scenarios" flowing back and forth through time. The scenarios are a virtual reality…comprised of dense and finely differentiated patterns in the brain circuits.
>
> Who or what within the brain monitors all this activity? No one. Nothing. The scenarios are not seen by some other part of the brain. They just *are*. Consciousness is the virtual world composed by the scenarios.

However, later in the book, a different Wilson emerges. In the words of the imaginary empiricist which he admits are his own views, he says:

> But to share reverence [for sacred symbols] is not to surrender the precious self and obscure the true nature of the human race. We should not forget who we are. Our strength is in truth and knowledge and character, under whatever sign.

Wilson cannot have it both ways. The "precious self" does not emerge from a virtual world of scenarios. The valuation of truth and knowledge and character does not emerge from scenarios—the latter just are. Nor does it do any good to imply that everything will ultimately become clear when scientists finally make their last grand synthesis. One recalls Kierkegaard's criticism of Hegel expounding a "system" that postpones all understanding to a final exposition that never comes. Wilson's view leads to a schizophrenic mind-set, or, perhaps what is more manageable for the mind, an attitude of hypocrisy in which lip service is given to the "precious self" while in fact devaluing its existence.

~ ~ ~

The progress of scientific technology seems to be matched by a retrogression of the human spirit. This phenomenon is nothing new; it was noted by Socrates with respect to the physics of his day. The desire for knowledge seems to be readily transformed into a will to power that is ultimately detrimental to the society. This tendency is not identical to the crude power desired by tyrants but appears as a subtler domination of the susceptibilities of mass man. There are many Cagliostros capitalizing on the magical powers of the laboratory to create an appearance of human progress. Knowledge as power is the watchword of the times. Scientific knowledge is hollow, however, when it is applied to understanding of the self. The more scientists pore over the minutiae of the brain, the less understanding and appreciation there is of this self. Finally, there emerges the ultimate absurdity, the denial of self, which when linked to computer theory results in a form of spiritual suicide—an unwitting suicide making the situation the stuff of tragedy.

A new millennium has begun with the world subject to American technological know-how. Things are firmly in the saddle, riding mankind to a degree undreamed of by Emerson and his contemporaries. The technological dominance of America is founded upon disinterest, disbelief, and devaluation of the metaphysical self by those who control the social thought-structure. It is doubtful whether this state of affairs can continue indefinitely. The American social landscape is volcanic, utilizing a metaphor that described Europe at the beginning of the twentieth century. It is unlikely that America can avoid equivalent upheavals. A nation, no matter how 'free,' cannot endure by technology alone.

How is one to live in such a condition? One needs food, shelter, and physical gratification. It is necessary to secure one's biological existence. Technology has a major role to play *but only in the service of the self.* Relationships, culture, and ancestral traditions all have their role in support of individual development. However, the inner self, the metaphysical core of a human being, needs to be protected from noxious influences no matter how superficially attractive they may appear. A metaphysical concept of life must direct the individual. In regards to the current materialist view of existence, it is pertinent to recall Hamlet's admonition to skeptical Horatio who had recently returned from a scholar's life in Wittenberg. "There are more things in heaven and earth, Horatio, than are dreamt of in your philosophy." One need not believe in ghosts to recognize the wisdom of Shakespeare's remark. It is necessary to constantly remember that there is more to human life than is recognized by the materialist philosophy. The interior self is a reminder of this reality; however, its voice can be drowned out by the cacophony of noise emanating from technological existence. And if this self becomes to be regarded as an illusion, to be equated with belief in ghosts and legends, then its voice will be silenced permanently.

There is a demon that haunts the appearance of creative expression. The demon prevents the perception of meaning to the independent expressions of the inner self. The richer the inner self, the more susceptible it can be to this demon that may be defined as the persistent need for societal approval. This need is manifest from earliest life by the need children have for parental approval of their creative activities. Teachers wield great power in the classroom because of this need. Later, it is peers and employers to whom this power is assigned. However, in most market economies, one symbol of societal approval takes precedence over all personal interactions. This is the pervasive symbol of *money*, which is the abstract representation of all values in a material world. Remuneration is the approval sign that dominates creative expression.

~ ~ ~

The way to exist in a culture in which money rather than the self is the primary value is through a rigorous process of "unlearning," a process that requires recognition of the reality and value of a self unconnected to fame or fortune. There are many individuals, many cultures, many ways of being which have disappeared without an historical trace. One cannot thereby say that their existence was irrelevant; one can only say that our society has not been afforded the opportunity of appreciating them. They fill a place in a continuum of being artificially divided by humans into time and space. They *were* and thus have meaning albeit it is a meaning not evident to us. It is foolish arrogance to imagine that what is not perceptible by us has no significance in a scheme of things beyond our ken.

The slogan "art for art's sake" is better rephrased to say "art for the self's sake." Every product of the creative drive has enhanced the self of its creator and thus has meaning. Without an understanding of this truth, works of art become entertainment for the philistines or scholarly estheticism for critics—not to speak of investment opportunities for collectors. It is the same for everything; the ultimate meaning of human activity from the first steps of the infant to the most esoteric artwork is the enhancement of the self, the fulfillment of the yearning for maximal development of the potential of the interior self. However, this development requires a faith in the instinct that drives it. Otherwise one is lost amidst the utilitarianism urged upon the individual by virtually every societal structure. One needs to remember that the ultimate justification of society is to foster development of the individual. When this relationship is not clearly recognized, the self is sacrificed to the endless utilitarian demands put upon it. It is important to have food, family, shelter, and protection but only in the service of the interior self. This faith is not subject to objective demonstration; it depends upon acceptance of this unique intuition that distinguishes the self from other living creatures.

Human life can be regarded as an art form in which the final product is the developed self. Goethe once wrote in a letter to his friend Schiller that he hated anything that merely instructed him without enlivening his existence. Every self-respecting individual should reject anything that merely strengthens his position in society or adds to his property without "enlivening" his interior being. This is the kind of outlook that a human being is meant to hold rather than the clinging to superannuated habits of bygone times. It is an outlook based upon the realization that there are more things on earth and in heaven than are dreamt of by materialist philosophies.

~ ~ ~

At its core, self-development emerges as a mysterious phenomenon, not explicable through the usual formulas of physiology and behavioral psychology. It cannot be equated with the instinct for survival since many forms of self-development directly endanger survival and may lead to death. Its connection with procreation and growth of family is often contradictory. Study of the phenomenon is difficult because it is impossible to define with any degree of precision. Does it refer to access to education, training the intelligence, broadening of culture, strengthening of character, or acquisition of skills? The list could be enlarged but to no purpose. The German term *Bildung,* referring to formation of the mind, for which there is no exact English equivalent, more closely approximates the meaning of the concept.

Efforts to construct programs for self-development usually lead to pedagogical techniques that miss the goal. No expert can provide an individual with the will to self-development or instruct him or her in the compromises made necessary by social compacts with family and society. An individual needs to maintain his sense of honor, however he conceives it to be. It is only possible to endorse the primacy of the desire to develop the self. Out of life's experiences, the personality of the self emerges. The principal task of human life is formation of this self from raw will and formless desires.

~ ~ ~

Belief in a non-material self, i.e., a soul, is the *sine qua non* of personal development. Otherwise, one is at the mercy of the societal order of things. However it is framed, society represents the material world while the inner self represents the spiritual one. Nicolai Berdyaev claimed in his writings that belief in God is one's "charter of liberty." He meant that belief in a metaphysical god was the only way the individual can be freed of the many forms of slavery grafted upon human existence. Belief in God, however, essentially means belief in spiritual reality; whether one expresses this belief through a concept of a supreme deity or the concept of soul is a relatively minor detail. The most profound religious thinkers have often come to feel that these concepts are interchangeable. The key point is to be conscious of spiritual existence.

Proponents of the materialist worldview have persuaded themselves not only that there is no God but also that a spiritual self does not exist. Like ideologues throughout history, they seek to convert the whole world to their point of view, albeit subtly and without crude measures. They are well on their way to succeeding with their never-ending programs of scientific investigation. Control of nature is the principal weapon of persuasion replacing brute force of former times. The superficial allegiances given to traditional, naïve religious belief cannot stand up to the powers of modern technology. The only means available to the individual to protect his soul is reliance on the primary experience of a spiritual self and a realization of the untenableness of materialism as a philosophy of life.

The goal of life as it emerges to the individual who can discern a metaphysical reality behind the smokescreen of materialism is to form his interior self. One seeks out experiences; experiences give rise to thought, thought to self-expression, and ultimately to reverence for the feeling, thinking, expressive self. This is a type of analysis of spiritual reality that is very different from the analysis of neuronal networks in the brain. It views material events as the outer representation of spiritual ones. It is the only view that can fulfill an individual human being.

~ ~ ~

Concluding Personal Postscript—The discovery of spirituality may come to one in various ways. My way has occurred principally through literary processes. Writing down my thoughts has been the means by which I have discovered an interior self. The defining moment in my sense of self comes to me when I objectify interior activity in written words. While experiences and reflection are the building blocks, it is not until I formulate objective writing that the real consciousness of my spirit comes upon me.

There is something about this process that crystallizes my sense of self. I know of no other activity in my life that equals it in significance.

The desire for public recognition that is often the consuming passion of writers seems to have passed me by, albeit I have been subject to other kinds of infatuation. Perhaps I have recognized its impossibility given the present state of the publishing world and the type of writing I do. But most importantly, the recommendation of Epicurus to live unknown is one that I completely endorse. It is the way I retain my freedom of expression. It seems to me that posthumous fame is the only type of fame suitable for the individual who wishes to realize his spirit through writing.

Others find different routes to the discovery of spiritual reality. Christians refer to finding Christ in their lives—the born again experience. The forest sages of India entered their spiritual life through intensive meditation in the midst of nature, albeit with minds prepared by prior philosophical speculations. Mystics of all types, religious or self-trained, have experienced spiritual states through the primal experience of nature, through meditative techniques, through physical exercises. The common denominator seems to be a consciousness that there is a dimension to the human condition beyond material bonds.

Writing is my route. Writers I have admired have commented on their motivation for writing beyond the material motives of fame and income. Max Stirner felt he wrote for the same reason birds chirped on their branches; it was a spontaneous outpouring he could not otherwise explain. Nietzsche asking himself the question in *The Gay Science* uncharacteristically could not arrive at an answer. Berdyaev refers to a 'visceral need' within him. Perhaps the most insightful was Fernando Pessoa who states if he had not written for several weeks, he became a different person and sensed the loss of his distinctive self. This is a sensation that I have often experienced.

I consider myself fortunate in that I have been permitted to develop myself through writing without the distractions produced by public recognition. This has not been entirely of my own choosing but I now recognize it to be a great blessing. I have been free to develop myself in this manner, which is the highest worthiest goal of expressive writing. I can honestly say that the number of individuals who have seriously read my work can be counted on one hand. I won't be so bold as to refer to them as "the lucky few" as did Stendhal of his early readers. (My literary destiny will not be that of Stendhal.) The lucky one has been myself who has been afforded the opportunity for self-development, something I would not trade for all the glories and riches of notoriety as an author.

It has dawned upon me that human life is a preparation for realization of spirit. I don't know how to otherwise characterize it. Experiences lead to feelings, feelings lead to thought, thought is transformed into expression. One learns to revere the entire process as steps in the creation of an interior self. Experiencing the expressive acts of others is a means of experiencing the spirit behind them. That is the closest that I can come to in emancipating myself from the limitations of purely material existence.

Morality to me is a secondary aspect of my spiritual development although I know it is regarded as its essential feature by others. This is not my experience so I cannot give it this preeminence. I am inclined to agree with modern sociobiological theory indicating that moral urges are a biological instinct, closely related to those of self-preservation and procreation. They are essential for species survival but to my mind are distinctly secondary to the development of a spiritual consciousness. I cannot understand the obsession of certain moralists with the preservation of life regardless of its condition. In the end, preservation of all life will lead to the degradation of all life. In my own case, I hope I have the good sense and capacity to act appropriately when my own life is no longer worth living.

Schopenhauer wrote that compassion is at the heart of all genuine emotions of love. One is entitled to wonder if he really believed this as he himself was hardly a compassionate person. Certainly compassion is a very human feeling and needs to be given its rightful place among the repertoire of human feelings. But when it is translated into action it is often the occasion of the most destructive results. Compassion rarely recognizes the best interests of others. It has often been noted that there are few more ruinous circumstances than the unrestrained obsession with another person. I myself never feel that I know what kind of help to provide the helpless and unfortunate. It is all I can do to manage my own life with a modicum of success. To me, there is a higher morality in this attitude.

~ ~ ~

It is my considered opinion that a dualistic attitude to living is the proper attitude for a sentient person. The concept of dualism is a bête noire today amidst scientifically intellectual circles but this is the consequence of brain washing by scientists. One's own instincts and experiences are a more reliable guide to reality than doctrinaire theories.

A person may need to provide for his material needs but this does not mean that spiritual awareness can be ignored. I think it is a fatal error to believe that biological or social functions, whether they be organismic, familial, or societal, incorporate life's ultimate values. I can imagine a cosmic master plan beyond my ken in which satisfying the necessities of biological life erects a scaffold upon which one climbs to the consciousness of spirit. This was Plato's view on the significance of erotic love. However, it is essential that the scaffold be not mistaken for the completed structure.

Nothing I have ever read affected me as much as Kierkegaard's confession in his *Point of View for My Work as an Author* that his entire literary activity was for the purpose of his own education and development—his *Opdragelse og Udvikling*, to quote his Danish. This single thought impelled me to study the language so that I could be sure of his meaning, although there are many other thoughts of Kierkegaard worthy of study. He is now famous as his thoughts have had worldwide repercussions, but I still think his own *Opdragelse og Udvikling* turned out to be the most important outcome of his writing.

Following the example of Kierkegaard's confession, I also do not wish to imply that I am no longer in need of further education and development. Although I am approaching the biblical end-state age of three score and ten, I feel my mind is just beginning to flower. This may be a dubious commentary on my own learning ability but one must make do with what one has. I have long known I am a slow developer. Additionally, I may have been more distracted than most by life's passions impeding my spiritual progress. In exchange, however, I have been endowed with an enduring vitality, which stands me in good stead. Perhaps it is the waning of the sexual drives that permits inner development to proceed.

Whatever, the reasons, I have been fortunate in retaining health and strength long enough to move forward in my course. Life still seems to me to be an adventure and I dread nothing as much as falling into a quiescent state in my own existence. It is horrible for me to consider the fate of Nietzsche whose mind I have admired greatly. His body far outlived his spirit. But there are other less obviously tragic endings that I would prefer to avoid. It seems to be that a principal feature of a developed life should be the knowledge of when to end it.

Regarding the question of the existence of God, which is in the mind of so many who aspire to a spiritual life or who are reaching the end of their biological one, I plead ignorance. All of my spiritual experience derives from my inner self. A "stubborn rationality" to use a phrase of Joseph Wood Krutch or, as I myself see it, my intellectual conscience prevents me from projecting this experience into an unknown deity outside my own self. It would be foolish to deny the possibility of a greater force at all levels of being which can be named God, but I know nothing of its reality. I would welcome the knowledge and at times have speculated about it. But as de Vigny put it in his *Journal*, all I have experienced on this subject is a vast silence. If more has been vouchsafed others, so be it. I can only express what I know. I have a suspicion, however, that those who claim to know the will of a transcendental deity are the victims of a widespread delusion that has caused much harm. The possibility of developing an inner self should satisfy the highest spiritual ambitions of anyone; all that is needed is the will to realize one's potential. No savior has ever appeared to help me with this task.

~ ~ ~

Should there be a reader who has come this far with my writing, he may conclude that it is insufferably self-centered. I would be sorry to displease him but it would mean the reader has erred in his choice of reading material. To be self-centered is the principal theme of this writing. In any case, I have not written to please, entertain, or edify unknown readers, as should have become abundantly clear in the exposition. I write to develop my own persona. The essential justification of the writing is the value it has for myself. In my hierarchy of values, there is none higher. A reader ought to realize he is peeking into a private affair that may or may not be of interest to him.

Nevertheless, I have made this writing available to others. I think it is because I desire to be perceived in my entirety. I fear being mistaken for somebody other than I am. There is a natural wish in every thinking person to be recognized as what he really is over and above the role-playing of daily life. No human being can wish to feel himself a hidden isolate as though he were a monstrous Caliban living outside the pale of society. Harsh reality teaches, however, that this all too often is the case. One often seeks recognition by an unknown God when meaningful human recognition has failed to occur.

~ ~ ~

"Contempt is the shield of the soul" is the title of an aphorism I created in graphic form some years ago. Its meaning has greatly grown in significance to me over the years. The only way my soul can survive is to protect itself against the noxious influences of society. I have rarely experienced any social or professional circumstances, any family bonds, any personal ties where sooner or later this was not the case. A shield must be hard if it is to serve its protective purpose; nothing short of contempt is often needed. One can—one must—allow other emotions to exist as well; compassion, gratitude and affection have their necessary place in the skein of human relationships. The proper objects of contempt are the bonds that entrap, not other individuals who have their own needs and motives. But without a hard edge of some kind, the interior self cannot develop. It is my experience that where there is no capacity for contempt, there is resentment and even hate, which are more destructive and less personally beneficial feelings.

As a person thinks, so he becomes. What one values is the most significant feature of his life. I believe a person is fundamentally free to choose his values although he may not elect to exercise this freedom. A person who does not conceive of himself as a "free spirit" will become enslaved to one or another of the many types of slavery that exist in societal life. The materialist worldview compels the individual to put his will at the service of the material realities of daily life. This is the mirror image of eastern philosophy that teaches that the painful material "realities" are what are illusory. My belief, however, is in a dualistic human condition; it is that my reality consists of both "fire and clay," spirit and matter, spiritual free will and physiological determinism. There must be a meaning to this peculiar state of affairs, albeit it is unclear to me. This belief is not founded on doctrinaire considerations but on the nature of my existence as I have experienced it. What a person comes to be, I maintain, is a consequence of his will to realize his spiritual reality. In this sense, his personality can be said to be determined by antecedent conditions. Free will means that his metaphysical potential is in his own hands. I believe that its realization is the purpose of human life.

RANDOM FRAGMENTS OF THOUGHT

It has repeatedly occurred to me that departure from the United States is a form of liberation that I badly need. Just as I could not fully develop myself until I left my parent's home, so I feel now that the same is true for my residence in my homeland. No matter how many conveniences and supports it offers, it is still a giant vise about my chest, impeding my ability to breathe fully. It is not objectively a bad place to be, it is merely bad for me at this point in my development.

I have felt this way for longer than I care to remember, but for one reason or another. I have not been capable of acting on my feeling. The time is coming soon, however, when I will act on it. It would be a great disservice to myself to live out my entire life in the country of my birth. For years, I have been dreaming of life abroad where I can finally shake off my swaddling clothes.

~ ~ ~

I have leafed through a book entitled *The Seat of the Soul*. The author appears to me to be a modern-day Swedenborg; but in order to interest me, a spiritual work needs to be written, as Nietzsche said, with the blood of the writer. This author does not write with his blood. He uses the method of descriptive psychology. I have no objection to some of his ideas; however, the book does not touch me. Like most new age writings, it caters to spiritually needy people of whom there must be very many in our technology-based world.

Self-expression is a very different affair from didactic teaching even if both deal with the same subject matter. It is similar to the situation with sex education; one can be taught how to avoid venereal disease but erotic fulfillment does not come from manuals of instruction.

~ ~ ~

Angst is consuming me—the sign of consciousness of an unfulfilled existence. Specific but irrelevant content of my worries: my legal process, publication frustrations, relationship, current life conditions. The world is dragging me down. I'm trapped by a set of bonds that I can't loosen. Is this a manifestation of an inner disharmony or am I really entangled in a miserable situation? It's hard for me to tell which is the truth—or are both the truth?

Do I need a new life to relieve me of this grim feeling? Right now, I feel as though I am just marking time, waiting for decrepitude.

~ ~ ~

Am rereading Kierkegaard. His message is what I need. I can identify with his state of mind. However, it is necessary for me to filter out the obsession he has to relate his metaphysics to Christianity. I see it as a bizarre quirk afflicting him.

My present requirement is to take as a duty the development of the interior self that I call my soul (I should not shy away from this term). I must escape from the U.S.A., an intuition I have had for many years. It is an essential prerequisite for the emancipation necessary for my self-development. I don't know how much longer I have to live so procrastination could be fatal.

I'm thinking about combining my recent writings under the title *Affirmation of Reality II.* I can't subject myself any longer to the disinterest of commercial publishers. Whatever need I feel to produce a book can be satisfied through the new Internet-based technologies. There is a place for technological advances and I see no reason to ignore them. My feeling toward technology is akin to Aristippus' defense of his visitations to the courtesan Laïs, it was not visiting her that was dangerous, but being unable to do without her.

~ ~ ~

The two abilities one needs to maintain through constant practice are movement and language. The former is maintained by games and exercise, the latter by reading and writing. Speaking is virtually worthless in the world of today. Neither ability provides guarantees of self-development but they are essential prerequisites.

The movement from reading to writing is a sign of interior development. Ultimately, I should like in my

145

writing to dispense with all the props provided by predecessors. I should use very few quotations. However, I am far from reaching this point.

~ ~ ~

It seems certain to me that self-development occurs only as a consequence of the effect of the surrounding world upon the individual. Nothing happens to one in a closet. The natural question flowing from this observation is to what extent the individual should affect his surroundings—qua individual. Jesus taught that no man should hide his light under a basket but should place it on a candlestick for all to see. Jesus, however, is not to be trusted in all things so the question needs still to be carefully considered.

It is one thing to write, it is another to "publish" in the sense of making known or disclosing. Why should one wish to publish? This is a question I have not answered to myself to my own satisfaction. Naturally, the question does not include profit-oriented or scholarly publication.

One answer—Altruism. Some reader may be enlivened by my writings.

~ ~ ~

Maintaining my will to self-development is my central task—especially as I grow older with the attendant loss of natural vitality. With all the best intentions in the world, it is impossible to move forward without a driving will to overcome the thousand and one obstacles life imposes on the pilgrim spirit. To permit weakening of the will is a formula for death. It is better to die through overexertion than have death creep up gradually so that life becomes death before it is actually extinguished. The credo of Jack London comes to my mind; it needs to be taken seriously, regardless of age.

Suffering with allergies, insomnia, and the accompanying malaise, I resist medications like the plague. Some voice within tells me they should be avoided.

~ ~ ~

I believe that most individuals have a covert—or overt—feeling of failure permeating their psyche. This is certainly true of myself when I closely examine my inner state. Laboring in society with success as measured by the world's plaudits does not erase this feeling. It is no accident that the Protestant world, which has dispensed with the confessional, is where the concept of universal despair has arisen.

This sense of failure arises when one realizes he has not made of himself what should have been made. I regard failure as a more accurate term than guilt because it is what has not been done rather than what has been done that is the problem. The Catholic approach to this problem has been the confession of sins even though the nature of these sins has been misleadingly projected into external acts. But no amount of "moral" behavior, no medals or recognitions, no success of offspring, no fulfillment of sexual longings, can permanently assuage this feeling.

The question of how to cope with this problem dates back to Ecclesiastes. Attention to the needs of the interior self, the soul, is the only remedy I can recognize. This requires not merely awareness, but also *development of a metaphysical entity*, one's own self. Denial of this entity is the great sin of our materialist society. It may well lead to its destruction.

The persistence of monotheistic religions, especially Christianity, is based upon symptomatic alleviation of the sense of failure in individual human beings. However, optimistic, rationalistic, materialistic attitudes to life do not address the problem of personal failure in people and are not conducive toward personal development.

~ ~ ~

"Humanity is an odd mold found on the surface of an insignificant speck of matter in the universe." This is the metaphor coined by a contemporary scientist investigating the nature of humanity. The insignificance of the individual human being, according to this researcher, is impossible to overstate. This type of worldview is the natural consequence of *materia*-oriented monism. One can empathize with von Kleist's suicidal impulses following his reading of *Critique of Pure Reason*.

How can any person with any degree of self-respect not have a metaphysical view of his own self? What a sheep-like society we are! We have sold our souls for a mess of scientific-technological pottage.

It is abundantly clear to me that there is no place for my writings in the marketplace. It is probably for the best.

148

However, I would have liked to have been treated with a little more respect by the arbiters of the market world of publication. If I were to derive any benefit from fame, it would be to receive a little more respect.

~ ~ ~

Having reasonably solved the problem of my animal existence, I am confronted with the problem of how to dispose of my remaining energies. The preoccupations with money, family, and health, with household routines, with media diversions have become tedious. What to do? How to live? What is *worth* doing? It seems absurd to have to rely on crises or manufactured diversions in order to make life tolerable.

Many would say I have no roots in my community. This is quite true but the raw fact is that I don't want roots in my community. I regard the community I live in with distaste. This is a most unhealthy situation but I don't know how to remedy it. My internal emigration is voluntary, I don't want to reverse it.

My brave thoughts of the past have abandoned me. Writing seems to be the sole authentic activity left to me. But it is not enough.

~ ~ ~

My depression has lifted. Again my path seems clear and worth following. My uplifted state of mind requires me to steer clear of situations I can't participate in, especially the culture industry that has not the slightest interest in my thoughts.

I need to obtain a vehicle with which I can reveal myself without having to ride the culture hobbyhorse. This is not difficult given the present state of literary technology. The main thing is to maintain my motivation.

~ ~ ~

I judge a society by the quality of the men it honors. There are always high-thinking men in any society; the latter's distinguishing mark is determined by the degree to which it honors them. The ancient Athenians honored their high-thinking philosophers; consequently, we regard them as a superior culture. Roman society is admired because they carried on the traditions of Greek thought; had they limited their accomplishments to conquest, we would view them today as we view the Mongolian hordes or the Nazis of the Third Reich.

Who can imagine an Emerson being recognized in contemporary America to even the limited degree he was in the nineteenth century? There is now no public for such a deeply metaphysical thinker. Consequently, at some future, more enlightened era, we are more likely to be lumped together with Vandals, Huns, and Mongols than with the eras of Athens and Rome. Our peculiar melding of morality with technology will not save us from such a judgment.

Random Observation: Is thought justified by action—or, action by the thought it engenders? I lean toward the latter idea. The purpose of human life, as far as I can see, is to produce thinking beings. Action and interaction produce the experience necessary to this end. Action and interaction that does not lead to reflective thought is a perversion of the human condition. The material consequences of action are side products, analogous to the use of animal dung as fertilizers.

Must I participate in the interminable selling and getting of those around me in order to live in the society? Must I sacrifice my self-respect? I think not. If my society is in no need of me, so much the better. It is that much easier to make my peace with the mysterious source of existence called "God" by those with a need for symbols. Symbols, I admit, are often convenient for thought (but dangerous also); therefore, I will confess wishing to make my peace with God and not with my contemporaries.

Writing down the above produces a deeply-felt tranquility within me. They are thoughts that were in need of expression.

~ ~ ~

It is essential for me to create a life with new experiences. I am living on the capital of old ones. I have no interest in my current circumstances and have nothing new to express. Mere comfort and relationships cannot sustain me. My remunerative work is without any redeeming feature for my interior self. I can foresee gradual deterioration of my personality if I can do nothing for myself.

Maxim: Experiences without pain are of little value in self-development. *Pathos mathos* (suffering teaches). This is especially true of experiences with other places and cultures. To allow travel to be insulated from discomfort is to deprive it of most of its educational value. One might as well gaze at postcards or picture books.

~ ~ ~

I note many discussions on philosophy websites about the mind-body problem. There are a great many theories floating about. What I think is essential today is a commitment to the centrality of self regardless of how it is conceived. I am more than ever convinced of the importance of reverence for self as contrasted with one's position in the societal world. The world would be a better place for all. However, the only way I can see this happening is by developing the intuition that the metaphysical self exists and has a place in the cosmic continuum beyond time-space parameters. This idea does not sit well in our materialist, causality-oriented culture. Dialectics is of little value here, neither are the dogmas of institutionalized religions.

~ ~ ~

The concept of "bad infinity" (*schlechte Unendlichkeit*— Hegel, *Logik*) interests me. Our present age suffers greatly from the bad infinity of endless scientific 'progress.' The constant elaboration of the picture of the physical universe does nothing to develop the self. Interest is fixated on the never-ending new discoveries in the sciences, which stand in the way of genuine interior development. The progress of a materialist world does not apply to the self; here one must move in a different frame of reference. There is a spiritual immobility existent in those whose lives are

152

devoted to material progress. Reality for them lies in the reports of instruments, not in the reports of their interior selves. Kierkegaard notes somewhere that it is sad to see a talented individual sell his birthright for the lures of the physical [or biological] sciences.

I purchased for 50 cents a copy of Joseph Wood Krutch's *The Great Chain of Life*. It is an insightful little work and further elevates Krutch's estimation in my mind. Of course, evolution is concerned with more than mere survival. Something special is developing. His witty way of writing makes the whole matter seem obvious.

I am unable to read most of what passes for contemporary philosophy. My mind just shuts down and will not accept the inflow of the material. No doubt there is a healthy self-protective mechanism at work.

~ ~ ~

Banality of Values—It is not particularly brilliant to note that our western society is dominated by four desires: money, sex, technology, and possessions. Older desires such as conquest, fame, or knowledge of God have become outdated albeit they still are to be found in occasional individuals. Most people must have a concrete goal for their energies. The real question is why such banal desires dominate in an enlightened era. It is my conviction that until people place the desire to develop the interior self above other desires, we will continue to see banal values predominate in society. I have no idea, however, how this might come about. Perhaps some sort of cosmic 'grace' might be hoped for.

~ ~ ~

I am not one to penetrate the world in an aggressive manner. My style is to remain bound up in myself and expend my energies in introspective activity. I have often thought that without the sexual impulse, I would have become a hermit. If there is no meaning to the development of the interior self, then my way of life is meaningless.

However, I believe my way does have meaning. I can see no other purpose in living than in evolving an interior self. All this emphasis on interaction and communication is another form of bad infinity; one lives to affect others who themselves live to affect others and so on in an endless chain. The fruition of life is in the individual; otherwise it is an absurd universe.

There is no logical proof of the meaning of the individual self; one must intuit its significance. I am always striving to clarify and solidify this intuition. It emerges from my depths; there are no revelations from elsewhere, no divine messages, no sacred traditions to sustain it. Therefore, I feel it must be an authentic awareness of being.

Illusion refers the presence of an idea about the material world without popular confirmation. Ideas about the interior self are not illusions because they are not about the world of *materia*. These are the ideas so missing today. Personal development does not occur without metaphysical concepts to point the way. If things continue as they are, human beings will become indistinguishable from computers and will be relegated to the insect world by some superior form of life, which must inevitably appear.

~ ~ ~

What I see as the original human quality is the drive to establish individuality, to create a self distinct from the environment, to form a microcosm in the midst of the macrocosm. This was Leibniz' basic concept. In this respect, humans are distinct from other forms of life, they do not want to swarm like bacteria; they want to *individualize* themselves. Whether one sees in his social surround tyranny, technocratism, pharasaism, philistinism, tribalism, or any other of the countless social macrocosms that exist, one wishes to separate from them in order to establish individuality. If one wishes, for whatever reasons, to merge with his surround, it is a perversion of his uniquely human condition. There are always tyrants and power-mongers who promote this perversion but they are not to be given credence.

Kierkegaard's great contribution to culture was to clearly separate out the microcosm of self from macrocosmic preoccupations. He recognized the priority of self in the struggle for metaphysical existence. He had the right system of values. Nothing else is of great consequence in his writings. He was too loquacious, giving unnecessary fodder to critics.

Approaching my eighth decade, I feel myself to be at the height of my conceptual and expressive powers. However, my body is rapidly descending along the downward path of the aging curve. If this is not conclusive evidence of the distinction between mind and brain, then I don't know what else I could say.

~ ~ ~

155

Retirement—Without independently generated activity, there is no human life, there are only mechanical reactions. A life of pure leisure, pure contemplation, pure relaxation is merely waiting for death. Better any kind of purposeful activity, even the most senseless than none at all. Better to make errors than to do nothing. Better to expend energy than to preserve it, waiting passively for who knows what.

~ ~ ~

The basic choice in the human condition is becoming clear to me. It is between spirit and *materia*. If valuing the metaphysical individual spirit is an illusory value, than all that remains is tribalism and maintaining the species. Individual concerns are merely vanity, self-delusions created by an overly active brain. Food supply, shelter, reproduction, maintenance of ecosystems, political organization—these are the only things that count. In nature, as is abundantly evident, the species is everything, the individual nothing. Human consciousness then turns out to be nothing but a survival mechanism.

Intellectual society at the present time seems to have accepted the materialist vision of the way things are. Thus, all the emphasis on interconnectedness. But if they are wrong, we will have abandoned the human birthright of a spiritual self for no good reason.

~ ~ ~

Why do I yearn for something more than my present state? What have I failed to realize? I think the concept of God embodies the never-ending need to relieve the Angst of the human spiritual condition. Materialist-minded people do not seem to suffer much with Angst.

As I deepen my knowledge of society, I am reminded of the remark of Thoreau who rejected the recommendation that he attend a local discussion club by observing that his problem was not lack of social associations but too much of the associations already required of him.

Better isolation with Angst than superficial, self-serving, hypocritical, materialist-minded interconnectedness.

~ ~ ~

I feel fortunate that I did not pursue my youthful interest in philosophy to the point of making a profession of it. I would have wound up as Nietzsche did, harboring an impossible split in my soul. He was too long the professor to be able to completely extirpate academic attitudes from his consciousness. Consequently, he suffered a psychotic breakdown. I don't have such a conflict, and, luckily, I have retained my sanity.

Recently, I read a quote attributed to the current Pope that touched a receptive chord in me, something that I rarely have with papal utterances. He referred to "the perennial youth of the human spirit" in connection with his own eightieth birthday—I presume he was referring to himself and thus had something relevant to say. His thought resonates in my mind; I do believe, regardless of age, there can be a perennial rebirth of the spirit. The problem is to know how to encourage it to happen.

~ ~ ~

I have not written for several weeks. The distractions of daily life have occupied my attentions. I should not allow this to occur because I truly believe that when I write my thoughts my life is elevated to a higher level. However…

Now I will travel to Mexico and will again have to suspend writing for many weeks. Is the experience of travel worth interrupting my writing life? I don't know the answer.

Had an interesting conversation with a man who is a member of Jehovah's Witnesses. There is something about his spiritual orientation that appeals to me although his conviction that he will have a better life in heaven is something I could never share. I tried to explain to him that reality is more important to me than pious ideas. Nevertheless, I prefer talking to him much more than to my professional colleagues or my neighbors. What we share is the belief that developing the spiritual self is the most important thing in human existence. How this is to be done continues to preoccupy me although he seems content with the conventional Christian formulations.

My intent is to place some of my writings on the Internet—perhaps in a personal web site. I have no idea what will become of them but I think this will satisfy my sense of duty that I should bring out my thoughts into public view. The likelihood that they will arouse much interest seems very remote to me. Perhaps if I committed some particularly dastardly act, they might be noticed. In any event, I am quite content with my plan and have no dastardly acts in mind.

Already, I feel purified by writing down these thoughts.

~ ~ ~

Had an interesting conversation with a medical colleague on the subject of non-material being. In a way, it was a mirror image of my talk with the JW man. This person is a man in his seventies, bright, articulate, and personable. He makes a point of following all medical advances in great detail and is remarkably familiar with an enormous number of medical journals. Meanwhile, he has a definite philosophy of existence; it is that all being is material and efforts to persuade people otherwise are total humbug. This view he offers in an engaging manner so that it is difficult to categorize him as a narrow-minded pedant (which is in fact my suspicion.)

He watches his own health closely and is a firm believer in medications for one's ills. Although he is lively and alert, there is something about him that reminds me of an animated mechanical puppet. I think he has missed some essential element of human life.

I should not be judgmental. I feel I too have missed some essential element in my life. Its absence haunts me.

~ ~ ~

If I do not write, the expressive side of me lies dormant. My personality ceases developing. The best aspect of my existence, my capacity to create meaningful thought, fades into non-being. I become a passive creature, one more cog in the vast web of life, whose reason for existence escapes me. My mind turns to low, ignoble ends, unworthy of my potential. No matter how glittering the appearance, boredom and depression are the final results of my life without writing.

~ ~ ~

I am in Mexico now. ¿*Porqué*? Because there is something about leaving the U.S.A. that liberates my mind. I am able to stand aside more easily from the milieu that formed me and realize my own individuality—my real self. There is considerable discomfort associated with this change, all the familiar guidelines are gone, but the resulting freedom is worth the effort. I don't think I will ever truly become the person I aspire to be until I achieve expatriate status.

The voluntary wanderer from one's homeland requires faith in the kind of self-development consequent to his wandering. A spiritual orientation is needed since the materialist world does not value self-development unless it leads to material ends. (I must reread *Wilhelm Meister.*) It would be wonderful if there were some sort of divinity supportive of my belief but I have never had any intimation of such. No Higher Being has ever revealed Itself to me.

~ ~ ~

My younger brother unexpectedly died last week—supposedly of a heart attack, but the circumstances were obscure. I had very little genuine relationship with him. His death vividly reminds me of my own mortality.

Although I have accomplished hardly anything worth noting in my exterior life, I do not accept that my life has been a failure. I have kept myself alive and functional while fulfilling my societal obligations—but as much can be said of most of the six billion people inhabiting the planet. There is nothing visibly distinguished about my life. However, I have created myself as a unique being who has risen above the level of a purely material entity. I believe that I have distinguished myself spiritually even though my society would think this claim to be absurd. Beyond all the societies and cultures on earth, there is a reality of spiritual being of which I am a part. I have my place in this reality. No human being could wish for more.

Where is the technological revolution leading *Homo sapiens*? It is clear that the benighted society of Mexico (along with most of the rest of the world) is struggling with all its might to follow the lead of the colossus of the north—all its protestations to the contrary. I wish I had the capacities of a seer to be able to discern the future. Or perhaps I do see the future and refuse to recognize it…the robotization of the human species.

Fate has not destined me to be a mover and shaker in the world. Still, I trust that my own destiny of self-development has meaning in the ultimate scheme of things.

~ ~ ~

161

I feel as one returned from the tomb. For the last two months, I have been consumed by problems with my health, my financial affairs, the chaos left behind by my brother's death. The real me disappeared, the metaphysical self that lends meaning to my existence vanished. The automaton, which is what I am without expression of the inner self, dominated my being. Finally, now, I feel myself to be emerging again from the sepulchre of purely material concerns. It is difficult for me to express the sense of relief I have when I realize my soul is returned from the dead.

It is sobering to realize how fragile is the metaphysical self. Far more readily than biological life, it is subject to extinction by the slightest adverse circumstance. But, unlike biological life, it can return from the dead. At least, this is the case for me. However, I need to be careful; one day it may disappear and no longer return, as was the case of the transformation of Dr. Jekyll into Mr. Hyde.

What is the metaphysical self? Its reality cannot be denied, albeit its forms may be veiled and its possessor unconscious of its presence. The neuroscientists would have us believe it is an "epiphenomenon" of the nervous system; but this idea, of course, explains nothing. It is a reality requiring direct confrontation, however one envisages its origin or fate. The enigma of human metaphysical existence is as far from solution as it was at the dawn of conscious thought. Since Schopenhauer (whose philosophical ideas have hardly penetrated popular thought), no effort has been culturally visible for its elucidation. This statement does not apply to Buddhist culture, which may provide a clue as to the attraction of Buddhism to educated westerners.

I can't allow the world to extinguish the real me so easily.

~ ~ ~

Again, what is the metaphysical self? I have often wrestled with this question. My thoughts on the question can be summarized in one phrase—consciousness of reality. The essential feature of the human condition is to realize this consciousness. All other human attributes or accomplishments seem to me to be of secondary importance. Other forms of life find their meaning in living out their natural lives; it is only humans who are impelled to develop consciousness beyond mere survival. I am aware that neurobiologists have claimed that consciousness is a survival mechanism as well, but this idea seems untenable to me. There are too many examples where the realization of consciousness is unrelated to or even runs directly counter to the ability to survive. Such a theory degrades the human condition.

Kierkegaard entitled one of his books, *Purity of Heart is to Will One Thing*. This matchless phrase underlines the importance for every thinking being to recognize the one thing of greatest importance in his existence. I part company with S.K. in deciding what this thing is but the concept is all-important. Realization of the metaphysical self is what I believe to be the one thing necessary in a person's life. Other accomplishments are subsidiary to this purpose.

I live in a society whose values are completely divergent from mine. There is an unspoken, but crystal-clear agreement out there that if there is one thing needful, it is money. Most other values—career, education, fame, and so forth—are secondary to this supreme value. A certain importance is given to family and relationships but in the end what most people wish for all the family, including themselves, is to accumulate wealth, the more, the better. Older values like religion, patriotism, morality, or political ideology are given lip service at best or indirectly subverted to the one thing needful, supporting the ever-increasing material requirements of life. Of course, the time-honored human emotions of friendship, compassion, and family bonding persist but represent instinctive phenomena, not to be compared with the higher level of human consciousness leading to willed behaviors.

Each individual needs to develop his own route toward the consciousness of reality. No apostle, no saint, no wise man can serve as a guide. There is no single path, no one achievement leading to this goal. Reality can never be plumbed in its totality; we puny individuals are not equipped to fulfill this task. One thing that can be said, however, is that ignoring the metaphysical aspect of existence will permit nothing but the most rudimentary consciousness of its nature. Physical sciences do not begin to explain the dimensions of the human condition.

Inevitably, one must choose between self-development, i.e., development of the metaphysical self, and development in society with its current emphasis on material technology. If one is not conscious of the metaphysical self, does not value it, and see its development as the one thing needful for a full life, he will be unable to do what is necessary to make it flower. His opportunity to create a full human being will have been missed.

~ ~ ~

Sooner or later, any person with a consciousness of the metaphysical dimensions of his existence begins to think that he cannot be an island of metaphysical being in the midst of an otherwise physical universe. He begins to think that there must be a larger metaphysical reality of which he is a part. The possibilities of this reality loom large in his mind and, ultimately, he gives this larger reality a name, which in the Judeo-Christian tradition is "God." Whatever be the differences and disputes over the nature of this larger reality, its fundamental significance is that of an intuition of a larger metaphysical reality beyond that of the individual himself. Those who do not believe in the reality of metaphysical being cannot really believe in God; those who do believe, find this belief easy to accept, albeit with a very varied expression.

~ ~ ~

I reached the age of seventy years yesterday—having been given the biblical three score and ten, anything more will be icing on the cake. My mind is far superior to what it was in the past; unfortunately, I cannot say the same of my body.

My Nietzsche book is in the publication process. It amuses me to think that in twenty years of writing philosophy, I could never find anyone interested in publishing my work. However, a scholarly work on a long-dead philosopher seems to be another matter.

~ ~ ~

My real self has been in a deep freeze these past few weeks. It has been overcome by the myriad of petty details of my 'affairs.' On top of this there is the matter of my failing physical abilities—natural of course to a *viejo* of seventy years.

However, I resist decrepitude and still have enough reverence for my soul to work at maintaining it in a proper condition. Age is no reason to surrender one's capacities for meaningful living. Spinoza says a free man thinks of death least of all things; his wisdom is a meditation on life. I must remember the implications of this thought. If I can maintain myself open for significant things to happen, they will happen. The important thing is not to become trapped in the myriad details of everyday existence.

~ ~ ~

Wer besitzt, wird besessen—This saying from Nietzsche succinctly summarizes my predicament. I am constantly being possessed by my affairs. Estates, home, finances, publication, *usw* occupy my mind so that it cannot dwell amidst the one thing necessary for my peace of mind. Discipline is needed to resist being possessed by possessions. I understand the Greek Cynics who viewed giving away possessions as an essential prerequisite to the philosophic life. (However, they did not marry.)

~ ~ ~

Rereading *Also Sprach Zarathustra*. Finally, I seem to be capable of handling the style and absorbing the content.

Whatever Nietzsche says about the nature of the soul, he writes as if it were the only reality of concern to him. My sentiments also.

I use the concept of 'self-development' for what N. terms 'self-overcoming.' They seem to be identical ideas; moving the self from one state to another is a form of self-overcoming. The main thing is to value the process above all else.

Trying to introduce my thoughts into the "world wide web" is harder than if I were to try to explore an uncharted Congo without guide or resources. It is beyond my capacities. It may be fine for arranging hotel reservations or buying air tickets, but to enter into with my thoughts! Impossible!

~ ~ ~

Random assertions:

Thoughts are the blood of the soul.

The metaphysical self called the soul *is an entity.*

Just as blood has many roles in mammalian species, so does thought have many roles in *Homo sapiens.*

The soul thinks—the highest function of human beings.

Valuation of spirit, disdain of *materia,* metaphysical conception of self—these attitudes distinguish the superior personality...dare I say *Übermensch*?

Problems of nomenclature—soul, spirit, mind, self, psyche—are equivalent terms. A multiplicity of terms interferes with the need for a clear sense of humans as metaphysical beings producing thought and values.

Not the brain but the soul produces thought and values; study of the brain explains nothing about these phenomena. However, the soul's expression in the world requires a functional nervous system.

Language is the sign of the soul; even the simplest naming process presupposes a metaphysical entity initiating it. How could one communicate with other souls were language not a form of metaphysical expression?

The obsession with maintaining the materialist dogma is the greatest impediment to personal development currently existent.

The only possible God is that of Spinoza. It has no relationship to anyone named Jehovah, Allah, love, or any specific being.

Thoughts can be expressive of utilitarian or spiritual aims but they cannot be both simultaneously. One cannot serve "God and mammon" simultaneously. By utilitarian, I mean all remunerative, scholarly, political, professional, medicinal, charitable, recreational, diversionary, culinary, or domiciliary activities. Whenever the word 'love' arises, I classify the activity as utilitarian, since it has to do with raising the temperature of the self's ambient milieu.

~ ~ ~

It should go without saying that the greatest events and the most powerful of experiences consist of bringing thoughts into consciousness. All the world's activities are trivia compared to the phenomena of the mind. What does Nietzsche's *Übermensch, höhere Mensch* actually do? He thinks higher thoughts—that is the mark of his superiority.

Anything conducive to thinking well is good; everything else has relative degrees of badness. The contemporary problem is that everyone is conditioned to think actions are the quintessential feature of living. And from there it is only a short step to think acquisitions are the choicest fruit of actions. Thus one arrives at a technologically based, consumer society. I maintain, however, that action or acquisition or anything else related to physical phenomena are only valuable insofar as they enlarge the conscious mind. As soon as they lose that facility, one might as well consign them to the ashcan of early development.

What is the significance of consciousness, devoid of concrete consequences? Here one enters the domain of intuition in which nothing can be proven or disproven. I believe that the thoughts of my mind have meaning in a larger scheme of things, even if they are without perceptible effect on the gross world in which I live. This intuition rejuvenates and exhilarates me and I have no inclination to abandon it even if every materialist that has ever lived sneers at my naiveté. They have nothing to offer that contains a better worldview in any sense of the term.

~ ~ ~

Visions of a Hyperborean—Non-explicatory, intuitional, mirror-image of *Subjective Will.*

> Let us face ourselves. We are Hyperboreans—we know well enough how far away we live. 'Neither by land nor by sea can you find the way to the Hyperboreans': that Pindar already knew about us. Beyond the north, the ice, the death—there is our life, our happiness...
>
> Nietzsche, *The Antichrist*

~ ~ ~

I must learn to transmute the petty annoyances of this life into something of value. Otherwise, the whole affair is hardly worth the effort.

Creating myself—the only goal worth having.

CREATING MYSELF—THE ONLY GOAL WORTH HAVING!

~ ~ ~

Nietzsche is the Christ-figure of modern times even though he was a man of the most modest personal capacities. His promise was noted early but he became a "little" man in every usual sense of the word. Not only was he marginal in his material resources, but his psychological resources were also marginal. He exaggerated, complained, connived, and wheedled friends and family unconscionably. Why then do I see him as a Christ-figure? Because regarding the one thing necessary, the development of his interior self, he was uncompromising and he sacrificed everything to that end. Writing was the route to his inner flowering. The tragedy of Nietzsche is that he did not have the strength to carry on with the path he had chosen for himself and he collapsed midway with the extinguishing of his metaphysical self. The title of his last book, *Ecce Homo,* is the fitting commentary for his life, as it was for his predecessor who died on a cross.

~ ~ ~

The image of Nietzsche has invaded my mind. It is disturbing to me—but also exhilarating.

~ ~ ~

One can form a dichotomy between the will to power (in which fame and acquisitions are subsets) and the will to self-development. I regard the latter as a form of expression superior to that of conquest of the outer world whether it be physical or mental in nature. "Reverence for self"—my key to a metaphysically distinguished life.

If Nietzsche had really assimilated this distinction, he might have avoided his mental collapse.

~ ~ ~

171

I am confident that I have mastered one of the most destructive forms of spiritual disturbance—the obsessive desire for societal recognition, even that extending posthumously. Tending the metaphysical garden of my inner self now fulfills all my aspirations. I can honestly say that my society has little to offer me vis-à-vis my sense of personal fulfillment in this life.

The problem I have, however, is being able to sufficiently direct my energies to my garden. The complexities of life and my sense of obligation to those close to me continually siphon off my limited psychic resources. If my life were simpler and less encumbered, I would be a happier person. It often seems as if my creative drive is not intense enough to overcome the distractions. I have not become *hard* enough to resist my society.

The only way I know to deal with this kind of problem is to conceptualize it, objectivize it, and seek a solution. If my will is not adequate to the task, then there is nothing further to be done and I must find my peace in the metaphysical desert of bourgeois conformity.

~ ~ ~

The will to affect people and the world (will to power)

The will to self-development (reverence for the self)

Two polar ways of living; the first evil, the second good. Robespierre or Marx versus Emerson or Thoreau. A Robespierre is always followed by a Napoleon, a Marx by a Stalin. The right way to influence the world is by force of example, not force of will. Morality is a negative type of virtue; it is not harming others, either directly or indirectly.

When self-development goes awry through misplaced concepts of self, inevitably the misdirected individual wishes to affect the development of others, i.e., the altruism of plutocrats or politicians.

My writing represents my self-development—period. I do not feel I have gone awry in this effort. However, I do not object to being an example for those whose inner state causes them to be attracted to my way of thinking. I would like my light to be at my door rather than under my bed.

All this has nothing to do with the social justice necessary to sustain human life on the planet. One must contribute to social justice as we are told by Christians, humanists, politicians, and sociobiologists.

~ ~ ~

I have been told in a humorous way that hyperborean means hyper-bore. Although it was meant as a jest, there is truth to it—as with all jests. For those whose minds do not expand in a hyperborean world, discussing it is a monumental bore. I do not wish to bore anyone; therefore, I prohibit all non-hyperboreans from reading these lines. Unfortunately, there is no means of enforcing this prohibition.

~ ~ ~

I have achieved the realization that no one point of view can define the human condition, or more to the point, my own condition. There are no universal truths available to individuals. One must be satisfied with the best and most interesting perspective that one's own mind can elaborate. In plain words, there is no "system" to rely upon other than what can be worked out by the self. I feel a certain pride in my point of view based upon my intuition of the *metaphysical self.*

Experience and expression—to fall back upon an earlier formulation of mine—is what is necessary for my development. I plan to be true to this formulation as long as I am capable of following it.

Extract from a poignant letter by F.N.—"Everything that I require as *philosophus radicalis*—freedom from profession, wife, child, society, homeland, faith..."—here are the ideal freedoms for a philosophic life. However, then where will the experiences arise that are necessary for self-development? This is a head-splitting antinomy worse than those set forth by Kant.

~ ~ ~

A dualistic viewpoint does not mean there are two different realities in the universe, it is rather there are two (or more) ways of confronting reality. The mechanistic way means concentration on the physicality of the external world. It is of course necessary for life. The advantage of this approach is in its predictability with the possibility of manipulating nature to one's presumed profit. The other approach is the metaphysical, which is the mélange of emotion, intuition, and will that compose the human inner reality. This is the far more interesting—and equally valid—approach that inevitably seems superior to those who cultivate it.

These approaches cannot be mixed without loss of the metaphysical element. The substance of a literary work cannot be analyzed according to grammatical principles. The impact of jazz is lost by confining oneself to the study of its instrumental techniques. Plato cannot be reduced to tables of categories. The metaphysical sense of reality fundamentally differs from the material sense; when it is reduced to quantitative analysis, all its meaning is lost. There is nothing incorrect about an analytical, material approach to reality; it is just that it is less interesting than the metaphysical approach. What is gained in security is lost in profundity. Pushed to the extreme, society becomes composed of talking robots and analytical machines. The distinctive human condition is devalued.

~ ~ ~

Note on Nietzsche's *Will to Power*—I find no way in which it differs from the concept of metaphysical self-development. The word "power" (*Macht*) was unfortunate in my opinion; it connotes images of societal brutality or unrestrained capitalism. Nietzsche's concept centered on power over the self, he felt this was the only form of power that counted in the long run. "Self-overcoming" was his supreme virtue. Power over others was a vulgar manifestation of weakness that coarsened the soul.

~ ~ ~

Why is it that I am so much more attracted to the outstanding nineteenth century philosophical writers than to the corresponding twentieth-century equivalents? I find myself largely disinterested in writings from my own era. There are no real existentialists in the twentieth century; there are only professors, storytellers, and critics. One exception is Fernando Pessoa who was far outside the mainstream and might be regarded as a nineteenth century leftover. Nor are there many writers in centuries preceding the nineteenth who have caught my attention. I have to return to antiquity to find personalities that interest me.

There is an interior breadth of spirit emerging in the nineteenth century that seems to disappear as the technological era gathered momentum. I doubt if its like will appear for centuries to come—if ever. Western society has paid the price for its infatuation with the machine; the price paid is loss of soul. How can a generation that disbelieves in the existence of the soul produce high-minded personalities? It defies logic.

Progress is an illusion of an era of "bad infinity." The human condition has peaks of development punctuated by long eras of lower forms of activity. The nineteenth century may have been such a peak; today, we live in the wasteland of a technological civilization best compared to the monument-building periods of pharaonic Egypt.

What a multifaceted genius was Heinrich Heine! It is apparent how much Nietzsche owed to him. How is it that all my life I thought he was a "lyric poet" without any acquaintance with the depths of his thought? And I a philosophy student in college! Had I known of Heine's prose earlier, Spinoza, Leibniz, and German idealistic philosophy would have been much clearer to me.

~ ~ ~

Novels are fine but novelists cannot write with their blood. For that, the writer and his writing must be one. Who can imagine any novelist today saying with Whitman that who touches this writing touches a man?

~ ~ ~

What is to be done? At seventy years of age, I have not been able to dissociate myself sufficiently from the business of practical life so as to devote myself to the philosophical (metaphysical) life. This ridiculous state of affairs is not due to the grip of unbreakable fetters or inescapable necessity but rather to a lack of determination on my part, an inability to take myself seriously enough to do what is necessary. I can see what should be done but have not done it. A familiar enough situation.

However, hope springs eternal in my aging heart. I have a remedy in mind. One thing is necessary, I must "be hard."

~ ~ ~

Nietzsche's hostility toward Christian metaphysics was so great that it overflowed into all metaphysics in his mind. But in fact, Nietzsche can hardly write two sentences without having recourse to words like soul, spirit, self, or similar metaphysical concepts. Nietzsche's "scientific" thought is really metaphysical in nature; he does not seem to grasp the distinction between quantitative science and metaphysical intuitions. What he means to reject are ideas like God, immortality, heaven, hell, angels, devils, and the like. When he says that the soul is merely another word for the body, he goes too far in his hyperbole. One never finds Nietzsche using the word brain or body when he means soul.

It is worth noting that the concept "metaphysical" is not Christian in origin but derives from the school of Aristotle.

~ ~ ~

I find making my way through the labyrinth of my own life to be the most difficult task of all. I am not sufficiently egoistical.

~ ~ ~

I note there is a correlation between periods of time when I do not write and the occurrence of depression in me. The nature of the depression is always the same, a feeling of ill-defined Angst, resentment, and unexpressed hostility. When I write, the feelings dissipate. I can easily conjure up all kinds of rationales for this phenomenon but the reality is I do not fully understand it.

It seems to me that I must always be in mental movement. Some people have their sensibilities elevated through immersion in nature or use of alcohol and the like. This is not the case with me. Impressive landscapes do little for me and drugs produce either deepening of depression or outright anger. However, working at my writing table perceptibly lessens my tensions and elevates my mood. I am at peace with myself.

What is the meaning of my literary activity? This is a major issue in my life that *deserves* an answer. Whatever may be the answer, it must be founded on a critical feature of my existence. Psychologizing does not help me understand it. Even Nietzsche, the master of existential prose fell silent when he posed the problem to himself (*The Gay Science)*. Kierkegaard was more enlightening; he said all his literary effort was done for the sole purpose of developing himself (*My Career as a Writer)*. But what does it mean to develop oneself through writing?

In a poetic vein, I may say that when I write (creatively, of course), I am reaching for the stars. Divine philosophy is my personal entry into the heavens. Who can be depressed or resentful when he is sailing through the skies!

(Was it Plato who first said the poets always lie!— that idea must derive from his cynical old age.)

~ ~ ~

My spiritual mechanism is creaking badly—it is too alienated, too mishandled, *too old.* It may be time to consider termination. Inertia, however, will carry one a long way if permitted. The aging Pope refers to "the eternal rebirth of the spirit"—perhaps I will allow myself to think this can be true.

~ ~ ~

Another person can never tell you *how to* live, love, succeed, become secure, or any of the other personal goals people strive to reach. Another person can only permit you to experience someone other than yourself, which is the fundamental purpose of any relationship at any level. Through experience of another, the soul expands.

Whenever I hear someone telling me how to live—never mind the ultimate absurdity of wanting to *sell* me such information—I close up like a clam. But when a *superior* person opens their soul to me, oh then I respond like a flower turning to the sun. Living in a commercial culture as I do, such experiences are rarer than Baja pearls. Please, however, do not ask me my definition of a superior person. Some things cannot be communicated.

The ultimate blasphemy of western society is the commercialization of the soul. Let the money-mongers commercialize God, Jesus, Mary, Moses, or any of the other icons of a superannuated religious pseudo-culture. But it is really too much to do the same to one's sacred spirit. Without recourse to an axe or a pistol, one can only turn away in disgust.

The great error in life is to mistake entertainment, conquest, charitable activity, or acquisition of goods for the growth of the soul. Writings such as mine have none of these features for a reader; if he does not experience my soul's blood in them, he has wasted his time.

~ ~ ~

The thought of writing too much disturbs me. One must know when to terminate expression as much as when to initiate it. Garrulousness is a serious fault in a person when he has outrun his creative abilities. I feel the time is soon coming for me to call a halt.

~ ~ ~

Why I write is the most burning of questions confronting my *daimon*. I cannot attribute it to the usual motivations—money and/or fame with the various subsets associated. I don't need money and I don't want fame. After these preliminary remarks, it becomes more difficult. What drives me to engage in the consuming effort of writing? What do I want from it? Some years ago, I developed the concept of "objectivization of the interior self" which may be a descriptive idea but is not an explanatory one. Why would I wish to objectify my interior self?

When I sit down to write, I usually have a clear idea of what I wish to say in the form of notes and conscious ideas. On the subject of why I write, however, I have no clear idea and hope something will be forthcoming during the writing. Often, I find that when I write, new ideas unexpectedly emerge. But one can never be sure of the outcome. It is an uncertain business to depend upon the realm of the unconscious mind.

Since writing for me appears to be a kind of instinctive activity, perhaps I should turn to the realm of instincts in trying to understand it. I have an instinct for self-preservation that is a fundamental fact of my life. Formerly, I had an instinct to engage in sexual relationships with women who attracted me but, thankfully, that instinct has waned. However, there has been no waning of my instinct to write; on the contrary, it has intensified as the sexual instinct recedes.

I regard the desire to develop my interior self as an instinct quite analogous to that of self-preservation. One has a physical basis, the other, a metaphysical one. I see no reason to limit instincts to biological matters. My drive to write seems to me to be a part of the instinct to personal development. There can be no doubt that the effort to formulate my ideas is an essential part of my self-development. It is a drive I cannot ignore. I have learned from long experience that when I do not write for an extended period of time, I tend to revert back to the hostility and depression that afflicted me so greatly during my younger years.

I preserve my writings for memory's sake. When I can no longer write, I plan to spend much of my leisure rereading my own writings. Bound books are a convenient way of storing writings. I really do not want anyone else to read them anymore than I want to be observed during my daily exercise and running. If I like to organize my writings in a conventional form, it is out of an esthetic sense stamped upon me by prior experience. I like to write readable and grammatically correct prose. I don't like spelling or syntactical errors.

Out of habit, I have tried to present my writings to public view. There is only one reason, however, why I should continue in this habitual pattern. It is to pay my debt to the universe of books. I have gained much from access to the thoughts of others; the social compact requires that this debt be paid to the best of my ability. I believe in participating in social compacts as long as they do not make impossible the development of the individual.

However, I know no one can predict the fate of writings and it is the height of folly to attempt to force mine upon a reading public with tastes far removed from my own. The most that can be done is to make them available to those who might be interested. There is no surer road to debasement in a writer than to become too involved with the fate of his writings.

~ ~ ~

The development of the interior self is not only a matter of self-expression. At least as important is self-defense against the assaults of societies that have no interest in the individual except insofar as he provides something valued by them. Services, goods, wealth, entertainment—these are the criteria by which an individual is judged in the current world. The defense of "freedom" that was the preoccupation of so many thinkers in former times is no longer a significant issue in materialist societies. Those with aberrant ideas are not persecuted; they are merely ignored. Of far greater importance is the question of how the individual can form his own soul in societies that no longer believe in its existence.

In order to survive as a metaphysical being, the individual needs to learn how to defend himself psychologically against an overwhelmingly materialist culture. It is not enough to ensure one's daily bread; the soul must be defended as well. The pressures of family, career, money (the basic symbol of a materialist culture) combined with an all-pervasive media constantly drumming materialist values into the brain requires an exceptional defense of the soul if it is to have any chance of success. Personal expression must not only develop the self, it must formulate a *contempt* for the base, spiritless world oblivious to metaphysical values. Without a properly directed contempt, one's soul stands little chance of survival no matter how high-minded the individual may become. Fame is a mental disease worse than psychosis, monetary wealth is worse than poisonous air. There are dangers everywhere; one must be exceedingly hard and cunning in order to avoid them.

Self-expression needs to develop the basis for contempt ahead of the need to enunciate positive values. As noted in antique times by Antisthenes, unlearning must precede new learning. It should not need saying that the object of contempt is properly not other individuals *per se* but the demeaning effect society has exerted upon them. Admittedly, it may be difficult at times to establish the distinction.

As far as God, love, religion, social justice, and other apparent necessities of the human condition are concerned, I put them in the same category as plumbing and politics. They are necessary factors in the comedy of mankind but in no way should they distract the individual from the one thing needful in his brief life, the development of his soul.

Thus, there are two emotions that I regard as essential for a successful life; *contempt* as the shield of the soul and *reverence* for its intrinsic significance.

~ ~ ~

The focus on the self as the essential reality is a universal part of the history of humanity. It composes the heart of

Vedantic and Buddhist teachings, as well as "mystical" elements in Jewish, Christian, and Islamic traditions. It is what prevents an individual from realizing his innate spirituality that is the key rather than religious, scholarly, or literary presentations of this natural awareness. There is an instinctive tendency to personal spirituality in every human being but the development of this tendency requires the unlearning of mental habits imposed by societal attitudes. Without freeing oneself from societal attitudes, personal development is all but impossible.

Every person is born into a particular set of circumstances that are outside of his control. These circumstances must be dealt with in order for the interior self to come to fruition. An adult human being has to free himself from the habits and mindsets of his childhood that serve as crutches until he can achieve independence. To hold on to these crutches in the name of loyalty to tradition, family, country, or race is to condemn oneself to perpetual infancy. Unlearning means to replace the blind beliefs foisted upon one by his milieu with his own self-realization. This is usually a difficult task.

Regarding my own self, I have slowly (too slowly!) come to recognize the soul-destroying values imposed upon me during my childhood. They are essentially the values of every *materia*-oriented, technologically-minded society with an added overlay of an immigrant family desirous of assimilating at all costs to this type of society. Money, property, and professional prestige were the basic elements of assimilation. These values were stamped upon my childhood psyche much as cattle are branded to establish ownership. Removing such a brand is all but impossible without the most rigorous reformulation of one's personality; even then, the scars remain forever. This is not unique to immigrant offspring; there is no one, no matter what their circumstances and education, who does not have a brand burned onto them that they must remove in order to achieve personal development.

This is how I have come to realize that suspicion, contempt, and hardness are essential qualities of the developed soul. The positive virtues can only appear after one is freed of the burdens of childhood. Many people are incapable of or unwilling to shed the constrictive skin of their childhood. They remain imprisoned all their lives in the jails of their childhood.

Writing is my key to unlocking childhood fetters.

~ ~ ~

My spirit resonates with the words of Marcus Aurelius, "This that I am, whatever it may be, is mere flesh and a little breath and *To Hegemonikon* [governing principle]." The essence of my interior self is its governing principle, all the rest—emotion, intelligence, will—may well be the veiled products of cerebral discharges. But I sense my governing principle to be a metaphysical entity, lying outside the realm of the lifeless laws of material causality. I have declared myself to be independent of my physical environment, a declaration that can have no meaning to denizens of a purely physical world.

The *Meditations* of Marcus Aurelius (a title added by copyists) is the single philosophical work I endorse without reservation. Marcus has no theology, no system of metaphysics, no analysis of the nature of things. He is not particularly imaginative or creative in his literary style. But he pursues one goal relentlessly, that of strengthening and refining his own governing principle, a term that I understand to mean his soul. There is no point in again dwelling on semantics; I will always know what I mean and so will any reader who may have followed me this far. Marcus exemplifies what I understand reading or writing philosophy to be, a method for strengthening the soul. Some of his thoughts are not relevant to our era. Marcus had to deal with his role as Emperor of the Roman Empire, a weighty enough task, but no less difficult than my role as a subject of the Technological Empire of the United States of America. Marcus was not always an emperor, but I have always been a reluctant citizen of the latter empire.

There are those who say that *To Hegemonikon* is an illusion that is merely the consequence of former experiences expressed as a mystical concept devoid of reality. Like everything else in the materialist view of things, it is attributed to antecedent causes, which one day will be susceptible to neurophysiological analysis. So be it. It is fruitless to argue the point. It is not a matter amenable to logical argument. Every individual finds his own conception of reality, inclusive of his own reality. Those who do not intuit a metaphysical basis to their inner self will prefer atoms to spirit. However, the issue is not an abstruse disputation because it determines the core substance of one's life. "Either providence or atoms," to again quote Marcus; the choice that is made is a highly significant one. I think I would prefer not to exist under the conditions of the latter.

~ ~ ~

No one who meditates seriously on his life and on the world can avoid thinking about the idea of God. It is an all-pervasive influence in western societies. Somewhere Nietzsche says that the moment the term "God" appears, serious metaphysical discussion ends. As in the case of most Nietzschean hyperbole, there is a substantial amount of truth in the statement. I have no personal experiences to relate to the concept of God. There is nothing in it that corresponds to my metaphysical sense of reality. Once all the historical traditions and sentimentality of ancestral beliefs are set aside, nothing remains for me to grasp. Who is willing to say today that he has *experienced* God directly? Not the emotions connected to the idea, not the relief that comes from trusting in an all-powerful authority, not even the intellectual attraction of the idea of an all-encompassing reality, but God directly or immanently. Today, such are only to be found in institutions for the mentally deranged.

It is one thing to acknowledge the possibility of a power beyond one's capacity for comprehension; it is quite another to claim knowledge of its wishes or intentions. Yet one cannot take two steps in society without confronting such claims. The coinage of the U.S.A. proclaims the trust in God. What is this trust? Where is the derivation of this grandiose idea in a secular country? In fact, Nietzsche was right in his indignation over Christianity; the idea that any religious organization has insight into "God's will" does inhibit thought on metaphysical topics. One has to turn to ancient Eastern scriptures to discover what is possible when individuals think seriously about themselves.

Very little historical knowledge is needed to perceive the damage done to individuals by the major monotheistic religions claiming to know God's will. There is the overt and covert suppression of significant metaphysical thought, not to speak of the many instances of murder, torture, obliteration of cultures, and complete indifference to personal rights. It may well be that such things also occurred independently of religious institutions, but these institutions claimed to speak for God. Today, advocating torture and mayhem may have been suspended by Christian prelates; however, obliteration of personal rights continues in more subtle ways. One need only cite the disgraceful suppression of women's rights to control their own reproductive activity. Future generations will look with dismay on the effort of churches to suppress birth control and abortion but this will not help women presently suffering from such oppression. The past victims of torture, inquisitions, witch-hunts, crusaders, and religiously-motivated conquistadors are not recompensed by contemporary suspension of these brutal actions. The history of institutional Christianity is not edifying, to say the least

The concept of a divine "right to life" is not supported by the processes of nature, which include the species *Homo sapiens.* These processes, which are the closest one can get to evidence of a divine will acting in the world, have no regard for individual rights at any level of existence. The concept of the right to life is a human concept, elaborated by human organizations and subject to modification by them. There is nothing metaphysical about the concept, which should be principally related to the wellbeing of the society and is properly a matter for discussion by sociobiologists.

I am of the opinion that the traditional concept of God ought to be abandoned, except for purposes of historical study, along with other concepts that have proved damaging such as witches, hell, heaven, and metaphysical privilege for ecclesiasts. The energy that has gone into this concept ought to be redirected toward the metaphysical self, an area that is more suitable for human thought. As

189

Heine and Nietzsche recommended, it is time for the common idea of God to be consigned to the dustbins of intellectual history.

~ ~ ~

Marcus Aurelius reveals how philosophy is possible for the great numbers of people in the middle range of intellect. Only a modicum of education and imagination is required to appreciate his writings.

When I immerse myself in the exquisitely imaginative and far-reaching essays written by Nietzsche in his twenties, I realize how he could hardly avoid going mad at a later date. The gap separating himself from his contemporaries was too great for him to continue to overcome. I hope I have made some contribution to his memory by dissipating the myth that syphilis destroyed his brain.

~ ~ ~

A Necessity for the Present Era—To overcome the magnified sensuality, stimulation, and sensationalism of a technological time, it is necessary to intensify consciousness of the metaphysical self. What was adequate in former days is no longer adequate to maintain a consciousness of the interior self. "Simplify, simplify, simplify," the doctrine of Thoreau, is more needful than ever to overcome the temptations of the world. Here is a task worthy of the highest representatives of *Homo sapiens*.

What is needed is not more Edisons or Einsteins, but a modern-day Heraclitus. Our era, however, is unlikely to be capable of seriously apprehending a Heraclitean philosopher.

Discard, simplify, think, write—my four pillars of wisdom.

~ ~ ~

The highest value can only be reverence for one's own soul. The intellectual giants of the seventeenth century— Bruno, Spinoza, Descartes, Leibniz—came to this value easily as the materialist dogmas of science had not yet reached their ascendance. But after Kant and the technological revolution, things were not so easy for high-minded individuals. Great suffering was required in order to sustain the sense of a metaphysical self. The truly spiritual men of the nineteenth and early twentieth century all suffered greatly. Now, however, suffering is not enough. The soul is narcotized by the media, by technology, by the information explosion, not forgetting the older narcotics of alcohol and religion. It is lost in a labyrinth in which the exit is exceedingly difficult to discover.

A neuroscientist of note has recently published a book entitled *Descartes' Error*. Descartes made a number of errors in his writings, but according to this thinker, his principal error was to espouse dualism as a concept of reality. This position reflects the well-nigh universal belief among scientists and intellectuals that dualism as an explanatory frame of reference is untenable in light of modern science. The soul is a mere epiphenomenon devoid of the firm reality of material substance. Such an attitude, however, glosses over the fact that *all* knowledge is representational and devoid of firm reality. Learning about the universe through the senses or instruments attached thereto is only one form of learning and a shallow one at that. Another, profounder way is through the intuition of the self. Dualism refers to different types of knowledge, not to two forms of reality (perhaps there are even more than two). The world of the "I" and the world of "*materia*" may or may not be the same noumenal world—it is the approach that is different.

Although the senses give a quite naïve view of the universe, history teaches that the perspective of spirit is usually driven out by the perspective of the senses. It is only the elite few (why shrink from the term) who are capable of maintaining a metaphysical awareness. *Je sens, donc, je suis* is more persuasive to most than the original formulation of Descartes.

~ ~ ~

I am living in the city of Querétaro. My plan is to be able, without lacking the conveniences to which I have become habituated, "to live as solitary and isolated as in the most remote of deserts." Time will tell whether my plan is feasible.

Ortega y Gasset, whom I have been reading lately, says that before one can become conversant with metaphysics, one must have a metaphysical need. If this be true, then I should become an expert in metaphysics because my need is very great. In my private moments, there is little else occupying my mind.

Here in the Mexican metropolis of Querétaro, technology is absolute king. For all the family spirit and *alma* of the Mexicans, they appear to have given themselves over to the love of technology to a greater extent than in the United States. They imagine it will rescue them from impoverishment. However, the arrangement is a Faustian one; what they will get in conveniences and perhaps longevity, they will lose in the quality of their life. The Mexican sense of *alma* is clearly on the way out. There is something depressing in the tendency here to swallow the technological bait, hook, line, and sinker.

Meanwhile, I seek once again to form my consciousness and find my soul in the isolation of a foreign land. I have been told I should seek to find myself through developing new relationships. This reminds me of the comment of Henry David Thoreau who, when given similar advice, declined on the grounds he was made ill from the ones he already had. Isolation is what I need, not new social contacts irrelevant to my needs.

I have only brought Spanish language books with me. This greatly limits the possibilities of literary stimulation or distraction—with the exception of Ortega y Gasset, whose writings I am carefully reading for the first time. His viewpoint seems close to mine but with a large temperamental difference. Of course, he was a noted university professor, thereby restricting his expressive range.

An alien world surrounds me. But, in its depths, it is little different from the world I have just left except its alien nature is more clear to me without the obfuscation of habitual attitudes. The outer world should be alien to every spiritual individual; what is necessary is to develop the inner self in spite of an alien surround. *I and the World of*

Objects—the title of Berdyaev—is proper for the entire drama of individual existence. Ortega y Gasset says only God does not live in an alien world. I don't know where he gets his information about God; I haven't the slightest idea about anything pertaining to any deity. If such should exist, my guess would be his world would be a most painful one since it would have to include the entire human race.

~ ~ ~

'The tyranny of the laboratory' has gained dominance over metaphysics; we live in a philosophical dark age in which utilitarianism and ignorance reign supreme. Science is the measure of all things and has entered the sacred sanctuary of self, laying profane hands upon it. However, the laboratory has nothing to offer with respect to the understanding of the phenomenon of self. Poking about the brain with drugs, electrodes, or photographic techniques will never provide information relevant to the meaning of the mind. What serves to diagnose brain tumors will not serve to elucidate consciousness. The techniques are misdirected and irrelevant to the subject at hand. Meanwhile, philosophy deteriorates, as it cannot survive without a continuing infusion of metaphysical interest. Neurophilosophers with white coats are replacing the great metaphysical minds of the past. Metaphysics is equated with astrology or phrenology and no longer recognized by society as a valid product of the human mind.

The arts cannot replace philosophy as an effective vehicle for the development of the soul because, without metaphysical intuition, they become mere agents of entertainment with ever-greater emphasis on crude sensual stimulation. Today it is a cliché to say that sex and violence are all pervasive in the public art scene. With the dependence on technology and the disappearance of metaphysics, we are well into the era of anthill society.

Summing Up. The human mind is metaphysical in nature and only minimally susceptible to physical kinds of analysis. A need for metaphysics (i.e., self-knowledge) is felt by all people at some level of their thought. Historically, institutionalized religions have provided for this need but these are less and less suitable for the purpose. The one thing necessary for a person is to cultivate his own mind while simultaneously maintaining an awareness of self as different in nature from the physical and social surround. Above all, one cannot submit to the intellectual tyranny of a naïve monism that relies for influence on tinkering with *materia*. Ralph Waldo Emerson enunciated the principle of high thinking and plain living; in this era of technological dominance, his doctrine should be held high as a guide to a philosophically fulfilling life.

~ ~ ~

The publication process—which I have just painfully gone through—is a kind of a beauty contest. One parades his product on the stage of public attention to try to attract the kudos of the judges. If one is noticed and gains a prominent position, many material and psychological benefits are forthcoming.

What has this spectacle got to do with the act of creative writing? Not much, I think. Perhaps nothing at all. It is essentially a fastening of the world onto the products of the metaphysical self. Yet such is the weakness and neediness of writers that they cannot endure the isolation of their creative self and require external validation.

Random Thought. A society is judged by the metaphysical depth of the artists and writers to whom it awards fame.

~ ~ ~

The goal of my life has been to evolve from a "busy body" into a "conscious body." By conscious, I mean in possession of the fullest range of understanding and appreciation of the reality available to me. The existence of my personality, I firmly believe, is an essential building block of a metaphysical cosmos whose extent I cannot know. Yet I play my part within it.

The valuation of the conscious self is the *sine qua non* of personality development. Without this value, one is totally at the mercy of the societal surround, and exists as a helpless animal caged in a technological zoo. More than ever before, institutionalized beliefs and values stunt interior growth. The religious systems with which I am familiar all inhibit growth of self. Therefore, I have always tried to create my own values and mental structures upon which to base my life. They form a skeleton for my existence without which I would fall apart. Herein lies the whole meaning of my writings.

Guiding Aphorism—Trust intuitions, distrust emotions.

~ ~ ~

It is curious—but not so curious—that within the pervasive science and technology of today, spirituality is a burgeoning industry. Everywhere one comes upon enterprising individuals developing spiritual doctrines and recommendations based upon them. In evaluating these enterprises, the first thing I want to know is whether anybody is monetarily profiting from them. I am an absolute believer in the saying of Jesus that one cannot serve both God and mammon. What he did not say is that in this world, "God" (metaphysical consciousness) can never compete with mammon and always winds up in second place.

~ ~ ~

Thoughts about Nietzsche—He was endowed with a sense of the metaphysical nature of the human condition like no man ever was. He exemplified the split personality required of *Homo metaphysicus*. Like an imprisoned bird beating his wings against his iron cage, Nietzsche wore himself out trying to cope with a world indifferent to him. The fact that he achieved fame after his breakdown reveals the perverse nature of public acclaim; what it seeks after, it destroys. What needs to be noted is that Nietzsche left behind a unique opus revealing his real self. All intelligent littérateurs recognize his uniqueness, thus the enormous fame that has come to him.

The metaphysical self has no connection to any societal, familial, or cultural institutions. Consequently, one cannot look to any of these areas of human activity to support it. The metaphysical self is a product of metaphysical forces that by their nature are unseen and unheard. Just as a fruit tree produces, in its own good time, a harvest of fruit, so the metaphysical forces of the universe produce, in their own good time, a metaphysical human being. However, they are not as reliable or productive as fruit trees so that a human being with a developed metaphysical self is a rare event. It is ironical that philosophers for ages have sought after the truth when what they should have been seeking after was the formation of their own souls. The ultimate truth of things may not be available to *Homo sapiens* but the creation of a metaphysical self is a task for which he is completely equipped.

My own plans at present include reading less, writing more, and exercising often. I am beginning to see my reading as a kind of stimulant to which I expose myself excessively. It is a lifelong habit, harder to control than indulgence in alcohol, food, or other stimulants. It must be controlled, however, if my interior self is to come to fruition.

Currently, I am exiled in a little village on the outskirts of Querétaro, Mexico. It is what I have wanted for a long time but now I must learn how to make the most of it. To repeat, think more, write much, exercise often, read little, eat sparingly, and learn to live apart from the materialist world. This is a large order for someone of my age.

~ ~ ~

As I recall (without my library), Xenophon's Socrates is said to have thought he grew better day by day through living the philosophic life. So should all men think, philosophers or otherwise. And so should I.

Any time you relish the plaudits of your confreres, any time fame lays hold of you through the attentions of the media, any time you bask in the warmth of family togetherness, any time you give way to *la grande passion* of whatever type, you can be sure your metaphysical self is sitting alone and neglected in some closet of your mind.

Fernando Pessoa wrote of his epic work *O Livro do Desassossêgo (The Book of Discontent)* that it was an *autobiografia sem factos*—an autobiography without acts (facts?). But the only kind of autobiography worth writing is that of the thinking mind, as Pessoa well knew. Acts and facts are of minor interest and should be left to biographers.

I will no longer attempt organized writings with chapters, parts, sections, etc. The effort is harmful to me and not conducive to genuine expression. All my writings express a metaphysical *desassossêgo* and are far removed from any form of didacticism. Metaphysics is absolutely the last place where professional formats should be utilized. Away with all introductions, lessons, outlines, and especially textbooks of metaphysics! Creative discontent is the proper form of expression for the individual concerned for his soul amidst a world of science and *materia*.

END

www.ingramcontent.com/pod-product-compliance
Lightning Source LLC
Chambersburg PA
CBHW051957090426
42741CB00008B/1440